THE SECRET OF
POWER IN PRAYER

Charles H. Spurgeon

TABLE OF CONTENTS

Compiled from sermons 328, 2002, 1103 and 507 of Charles Spurgeon.

Chapter 1
TRUE PRAYER-TRUE POWER!

"Therefore I say unto you, whatever things you ask, when you pray, believe that you receive them, and you shall have them."
Mark 11:24 (NKJV).

This verse has something to do with the faith of miracles; but I think it has far more reference to the miracle of faith. We shall at any rate, this morning, consider it in that light. I believe that this text is the inheritance not only of the apostles, but of all those who walk in the faith of the apostles, believing in the promises of the Lord Jesus Christ. The advice which Christ gave to the twelve and to His immediate followers is repeated to us in God's Word this morning. May we have divine grace to constantly obey it! "What things soever you desire, when you pray, believe that you receive them, and you shall have them." How many persons there are who complain that they do not enjoy prayer; they do not neglect it, for they dare not! But they would neglect it if they dared, so far are they from finding any pleasure therein. And have we not to lament that sometimes the chariot wheels are taken off, and we drive right heavily when we are in supplication? We spend the time allotted, but we rise from our knees unrefreshed, like a man who has lain upon his bed, but has not slept so as to really recover his strength. When the time comes round again, conscience drives us to our knees, but there is no sweet fellowship with God; there is no telling out of our needs to Him in the firm conviction that He will supply them! After having gone again through a certain round of customary utterances, we rise from our knees, perhaps more troubled in conscience, and more distressed in mind than we were before! There are many Christians, I think, who have to complain of this-that they pray not so much because it is a blessed thing to be allowed to draw near to God, as because they must pray because it is their duty, because they feel that if they did not, they would lose one of the sure evidences of their being Christians! Brothers and sisters, I do not condemn you, but at the same time, if I may be the means of lifting you up, this morning, from so low a state of

3

grace into a higher and healthier atmosphere, my soul shall be exceedingly glad! If I can show you a more excellent way, if from this time forth you may come to look at prayer as one of the most delightful exercises of your life, if you shall come to esteem it more than your necessary food, and to value it as one of heaven's best luxuries, surely I shall have answered a great end and you shall have to thank God for a great blessing!

Give me, then, your attention while I beg you, first, to look at the text; secondly, to look about you; and then, to look above you.

I. First, LOOK AT THE TEXT. If you look at it carefully, I think you will perceive the essential qualities which are necessary to any great success and prevalence in prayer. According to our Savior's description of prayer, there should always be some definite objectives for which we should plead. He speaks of things-"What things you desire." It seems, then, that He did nòt think that God's children would go to Him to pray when they had nothing to pray for! Another essential qualification of prayer is earnest desire, for the Master supposes here, that when we pray we have desires. Indeed it is not prayer, it may be something like prayer, the outward form or the bare skeleton, but it is not the living thing, the all-prevailing, almighty thing called prayer unless there is fullness and overflowing of desires! Observe, too, that faith is an essential quality of successful prayer "Believe that you receive them." You cannot pray so as to be heard in heaven, and answered to your soul's satisfaction unless you believe that God really hears and will answer you! One other qualification appears here upon the very surface, namely that a realizing expectation should always go with a firm faith "Believe that you receive them." Not merely believe that "you shall," but believe that "you do" receive them-count them as if they were received; reckon them as if you already had them, and act as if you had them-act as if you were sure you would have them. "Believe that you receive them, and you shall have them." Let us review these four qualities, one by one.

To make prayer of any value, there should be definite objectives for which to plead. My brothers and sisters, we often ramble in our prayers after this, that, and the other, and we get nothing because in each we do not really desire anything. We chatter about many subjects, but the soul does not concentrate itself upon any one objective. Do you not sometimes fall on your knees without thinking beforehand what you mean to ask God for? You do so as a matter of habit, without any motion of your heart! You are like a man who goes to a shop, and does not know what articles he would buy; he may, perhaps, make a happy purchase when he is there, but certainly it is not a wise plan to adopt. And so the Christian in prayer may afterwards attain to a real desire, and get his end, but how much better would he spend if, having prepared his soul by consideration and self-examination, he came to God for an objective at which he was about to aim with a real request? Did we ask for an audience at Her Majesty's court, we would be expected to reply to the question, "What do you wish to see her for?" We would not be expected to go into the presence of Royalty, and then to think of some petition after we came there! Even so with the child of God; he should be able to answer the great question, "What is your petition, and what is your request, and it shall be done unto you." Imagine an archer shooting with his bow, and not knowing where the mark is! Would he be likely to have success? Imagine a ship on a voyage of discovery putting to sea without the captain, having any idea of what he was looking for! Would you expect that he would come back heavily laden either with the discoveries of science, or with treasures of gold? In everything else you have a plan; you do not go to work without knowing that there is something that you planned to make. How is it that you go to God without knowing what you design to have? If you had some objective, you would never find prayer to be a dull and heavy work! I am persuaded that you would long for it! You would say, "I have something that I need. Oh that I could draw near my God and ask Him for it! I have a need, I want to have it satisfied; I long till I can get alone, that I may pour out my heart before Him, and ask Him for this great thing after which my soul so earnestly pants." You will find it more helpful to your prayers, if you have some objectives at which you aim and I think, also, if you have some persons whom you will mention. Do not merely plead with God for sinners in general, but always mention some in particular. If you are a Sunday school teacher, don't simply ask that your class may be blessed, but pray for your children definitely by name before the Most High. And if there is a mercy in your household that you crave, don't go in a round-about way, but be simple and direct in your pleadings with God. When you pray to Him, tell Him what you need. If you have not money enough, if you are in poverty, if you are in straits, state the case. Use no mock modesty with God! Come at once to the point-speak honestly with Him-He needs no beautiful penny phrases such as men will constantly use when they don't like to say right out what they mean. If you need either a temporal or spiritual mercy, say so! Don't ransack the

Bible to find out words in which to express it; express your needs in the words which naturally suggest themselves to you. They will be the best words, depend upon it. Abraham's words were the best for Abraham, and yours will be the best for you. You need not study all the texts in Scripture to pray just as Jacob and Elijah did, using their expressions. If you do, you will not imitate them; you may imitate them literally and servilely, but you lack the soul that suggested and animated their words. Pray in your own words. Speak plainly to God. Ask at once for what you need. Name persons, name things, and make a straight aim at the objective of your supplications, and I am sure you will soon find that the weariness and dullness of which you often complain in your intercessions, will no more fall upon you-or at least not so habitually as it has up to now done.

"But," says one, "I do not feel that I have any special objectives for which to pray." Ah, my dear brother, I know not who you are, or where you live, to be without special objectives for prayer! I find that every day brings either its need or its trouble, and that I have, every day, something to tell my God. But if we had not a trouble, my dear brothers and sisters; if we had attained to such a height in grace that we had nothing to ask for, do we love Christ so much that we have no need to pray that we may love Him more? Have we so much faith that we have ceased to cry, "Lord, increase it"? You will always, I am sure, by a little self-examination, soon discover that there is some legitimate objective for which you may knock at mercy's door and cry, "Give me, Lord, the desire of my heart!" But if you have not any desire, you have but to ask the first tried Christian that you meet, and he will tell you of one. "Oh," he will reply to you, "if you have nothing to ask for yourself, pray for me! Ask that a sick wife may be recovered; pray that the Lord would lift up the light of His countenance upon a desponding heart; ask that the Lord would send help to some minister who has been laboring in vain, and spending his strength for nothing." When you have done for yourself, plead for others! And if you cannot meet with one who can suggest a theme, look on this huge Sodom, this city like another Gomorrah lying before you! Carry it constantly in your prayers before God and cry, "Oh that London may live before You; that its sin may be stayed; that its righteousness may be exalted; that the God of the earth may get unto Himself much people out of this city!"

Equally necessary is it with a definite objective for prayer that there should be an earnest desire for its attainment. "Cold prayers," says an old divine, "ask for a denial." When we ask the Lord coolly, and not fervently, we do, as it were, stop His hand and restrain Him from giving us the very blessing we pretend that we are seeking! When you know what you need, your soul must become so possessed with the value of that device-with your own excessive need for it, with the danger which you will be in unless that device should not be granted-that you will be compelled to plead for it as a man pleads for his life! There was a beautiful illustration of true prayer addressed to man in the conduct of two noble ladies whose husbands were condemned to die, and were about to be executed. When they came before King George, and supplicated for their pardon, the king rudely and cruelly repulsed them. George the First; it was like his very nature! And when they pleaded yet again, and again, and again, they could not be gotten to rise from their knees. They had actually to be dragged out of court, for they would not retire until the king had smiled upon them and told them that their husbands would live. Alas, they failed, but they were noble women for their perseverance in thus pleading for their husbands' lives. That is the way for us to pray to God; we must have such a desire for the thing we need, that we will not rise until we have it-but in submission to His divine will, nevertheless. Feeling that the thing we ask for cannot be wrong, and that He, Himself, has promised it, we have resolved it must be given, and if not given, we will plead the promise again and again, till heaven's gates shall shake before our pleas shall cease! No wonder that God has not blessed us much of late because we are not fervent in prayer as we should be! Oh, those cold-hearted prayers that die upon the lips-those frozen supplications-they do not move men's hearts-how should they move God's heart? They do not come from our own souls; they do not well up from the deep secret springs of our inmost heart and, therefore, they cannot rise up to Him who only hears the cry of the soul-before whom hypocrisy can weave no veil, or formality practice any disguise! We must be earnest; otherwise we have no right to hope that the Lord will hear our prayer.

And surely, my brothers and sisters, it were enough to restrain all lightness, and compel an unceasing earnestness, did we apprehend the greatness of the Being before whom we plead! Shall I come into Your presence, O my God, and mock You with cold-hearted words? Do the angels veil their faces before You and shall I be content to prattle through a form with no soul and no heart? Ah, my brothers and sisters, we little know how many of our prayers are an abomination unto the Lord! It would be an abomination to you, and to me, to hear men ask us in the streets, as if they did not need what they asked for. But have we not done the same to God? Has not that which is heaven's greatest gift to man become to us a dry dead duty? It was said of John Bradford, that he had a peculiar art in prayer, and when asked for his secret, he said, "When I know what I need, I always stay on that prayer until I feel that I have pleaded it with God, and until God and I have had dealings with each other upon it. I never go on to another petition till I have gone through the first." Alas, for some men who begin, "Our Father which are in heaven, hallowed be Your name;" and before they have realized the adoring thought-"hallowed be Your name"-they have begun to repeat the next words-"Your kingdom come." Then perhaps something strikes their mind, "Do I really wish His kingdom to come? If it were to come now, where would I be?" And while they are thinking of that, their voice is going on with, "Your will be done on earth as it is in heaven." So they jumble up their prayers and run the sentences together! Oh, stay at each one till you have really prayed it! Do not try to put two arrows on the string at once-they will both miss! He who would load his gun with two charges cannot expect to be successful! Discharge one shot, first, and then load again. Plead once with God, and prevail, and then plead again! Get the first mercy, and then go again for the second; do not be satisfied with running the colors of your prayers into one another till there is no picture to look at but just a huge daub a smear of colors badly laid on! Look at the Lord's Prayer itself. What clear, sharp outlines there are in it. There are certain definite mercies, and they do not run into one another. There it stands, and as you look at the whole, it is a magnificent picture; not confusion, but beautiful order. Be it so with your prayers! Stay on one till you have prevailed with that, and then go on to the next. With definite objectives, and with fervent desires mixed together, there is the dawning of hope that you shall prevail with God.

But again-these two things would not avail if they were not mixed with a still more essential and divine quality, namely, a firm faith in God. Brothers and sisters, do you believe in prayer? I know you pray because you are God's people. But do you believe in the power of prayer? There are a great many Christians who do not. They think it is a good thing, and they believe that sometimes it does wonders, but they do not think that prayer, real prayer, is always successful. They think that its effect depends upon many other things, but that it has not any essential quality or power in itself. Now, my own soul's conviction is that prayer is the grandest power in the entire universe-that it has a more omnipotent force than electricity, attraction, gravitation or any other of those secret forces which men have called by names, but which they do not understand! Prayer has as tangible, as true, as sure, as invariable an influence over the entire universe as any of the laws of matter! When a man really prays, it is not a question whether God will hear him or not-He must hear him, not because there is any compulsion in the prayer, but there is a sweet and blessed compulsion in the promise. God has promised to hear prayer, and He will keep His promise! As He is the most high and true God, He cannot deny Himself. Oh, to think of this! That you, a puny man, may stand here and speak to God and through God may move all the worlds! Yet when your prayer is heard, creation will not be disturbed; though the grandest ends are answered, providence will not be disarranged for a single moment! Not a leaf will fall earlier from the tree; not a star will stray in its course; nor one drop of water trickle more slowly from its fountain-all will go on the same, and yet your prayer will have effected everything! It will speak to the decrees and purposes of God as they are being daily fulfilled; and they will all shout to your prayer, and cry, "You are our brother! We are decrees and you a prayer; but you are yourself a decree, as old, as sure, as ancient as we are." Our prayers are God's decrees in another shape! The prayers of God's people are but God's promises breathed out of living hearts, and those promises are the decrees only put into another form and fashion! Do not say, "How can my prayers affect the decrees?" They cannot, except in so much that your prayers are decrees, and that as they come out, every prayer that is inspired of the Holy Spirit unto your soul is as omnipotent and as eternal as that decree which said, "Let there be light, and there was light." Or as that decree which chose His people, and ordained their redemption by the precious blood of Christ! You have power in prayer, and you stand today among the most potent ministers in the universe who God has made. You have power over angels; they will fly at your will. You have power over fire and water and the elements of earth; you have power to make your voice heard beyond the stars! Where the thunders die out in silence, your voice shall wake the echoes of eternity. The ears of God, Himself, shall listen, and the hands of God shall yield to your will! He bids you cry, "Your will be done," and your will shall be done! When you can plead His promise, then your will is His will!

Seems it not, my dear friends, an amazing thing to have such a power in one's hands as to be able to pray? You have sometimes heard of men who pretended to have a weird and mystic might by which they could call up spirits from the vast deep-by which they could make showers of rain, or stop the sun. It was all a figment of the fancy, but were it true, the Christian is a greater magician, still! If he has but faith in God, there is nothing impossible to him! He shall be delivered out of the deepest waters, he shall be rescued out of the sorest troubles, in famine he shall be fed, in pestilence he shall go unscathed, amidst calamity he shall walk firm and strong, in war he shall be always shielded, and in the day of battle he shall lift up his head if he can but believe the promise and hold it up before God's eyes and plead it with the spell of unfaltering reliance! There is nothing, I repeat it, there is no force so tremendous, no energy so marvelous, as the energy with which God has endowed every man, who like Jacob can wrestle, like Israel can prevail with Him in prayer! But we must have faith in this; we must believe prayer to be what it is, or else it is not what it should be. Unless I believe my prayer to be effectual, it will not be, for on my faith will it, to a great extent, depend. God may give me the mercy even when I have not faith-that will be His own sovereign grace, but He has not promised to do it. But when I have faith, and can plead the promise with earnest desire, it is no longer a probability as to whether I shall get the blessing, or whether my will shall be done! Unless the Eternal will swerve from His Word, unless the oath which He has given shall be revoked, and He Himself shall cease to be what He is, "We know that we have the petitions that we desired of Him."

And now to mount one step higher. Together with definite objectives, fervent desires, and strong faith in the efficacy of prayer, there should be and, oh, may divine grace make it so with us-there should be mingled a realizing expectation! We should be able to count over the mercies before we have received them, believing that they are on the road. Reading the other day in a sweet little book which I would commend the attention of you all, written by an American author who seems to know the power of prayer thoroughly, and to whom I am indebted for many good things-a little book called The Still Hour, [Austin Phelps - 1820-1890] I met with a reference to a passage in the Book of Daniel, the 10th chapter, I think, where, as he says, the whole machinery of prayer seems to be laid bare. Daniel is on his knees in prayer, and Michael the archangel comes to him. He talks with him, and tells him that as soon as ever Daniel began to set his heart to understand and to chasten himself before God, his words were heard, and the Lord had dispatched the angel. Then he tells him in the most business-like manner in the world, "I should have been here before, but the Prince of Persia withstood me, nevertheless the prince of your nation helped me, and I am come to comfort and instruct you." See now, God breathes the desire into our hearts, and as soon as the desire is there, before we call, He begins to answer! Before the words have got half way up to heaven, while they are yet trembling on our lips-knowing the words we mean to speak-He begins to answer them-sends the angel! The angel comes, and brings down the needed blessing. Why the thing is a revelation if you could see it with your eyes! Some people think that spiritual things are dreams, and that we are talking fancies. I believe there is as much reality in a Christian's prayer as in a lightning flash; and the utility and excellency of the prayer of a Christian may be just as sensibly known as the power of the lightning flash when it tears the tree, breaks off its branches, and splits it to the very root! Prayer is not a fancy or fiction! It is a real, actual thing coercing the universe, binding the laws of God themselves in fetters, and compelling the High and Holy One to listen to the will of His poor, but favored creature-man! But we need always to believe this; we need a realizing assurance in prayer-to count over the mercies before they are come-to be sure that they are coming! To act as if we had them! When you have asked for your daily bread, no more to be disturbed with care, but to believe that God has heard you, and will give it to you! When you have taken the case of your sick child before God-to believe that the child will recover, or if it should not, that it will be a greater blessing to you and more glory to God and so to leave it to Him. To be able to say, "I know He has heard me now. I will stand on my watchtower; I will look for my God, and hear what He will say to my soul." Were you ever disappointed yet, Christian, when you prayed in faith and expected the answer? I bear my own testimony here this morning, that I have never yet trusted Him and found Him to fail me! I have trusted man and have been deceived, but my God has never once denied the request I have made to Him when I have backed up the request with belief in His willingness to hear, and in the assurance of His promise!

But I hear someone ask, "May we pray for temporals?" Yes, that you may! In everything, make known your needs to God. It is not merely for spiritual, but for everyday concerns. Take your smallest trials before Him! He is a God who hears prayer; He is your household God as well as the God of the sanctuary; be always taking all that you have before God! As one good man, who is about to be united with this Church, told me of his departed wife,

"Oh," he said, "she was a woman who I could never get to do anything till she had made a matter of prayer of it. Be it what it might, she used to say, 'I must make it a matter of prayer.'" Oh for more of this sweet habit of spreading everything before the Lord just as Hezekiah did Rabshakeh's letter! And there leaving it, saying, "Your will be done; I resign it to You!" Men say Mr. Muller of Bristol is enthusiastic because he will gather 700 children and believe that God will provide for them-though there is nothing in the purse often-yet he believes it will come! My dear brothers and sisters, he is not an enthusiast; he is only doing what ought to be the commonplace action of every Christian! He is acting upon a rule at which the worldling always must scoff because he does not understand it-a system which must always appear to the weak judgment of sense, visionary and romantic-but which will never appear so to the child of God! He acts not upon common sense, but upon something higher than common sense-upon uncommon faith! Oh that we had that uncommon faith to take God at His word! He cannot, and He will not permit the man who trusts Him to be ashamed or confounded! I have thus now, as best I could, set forth before you what I conceive to be four essentials of prevailing prayer-"Whatever things you desire when you pray, believe that you receive them, and you shall have them."

II. Having thus asked you to look at the text, I want you now to LOOK ABOUT YOU. Look about you at our meetings for prayer, and look about you at your private intercessions and judge them both by the tenor of this text. First, look about you at the meetings for prayer. I cannot speak very pointedly in this matter because I do honestly believe that the prayer meetings which are usually held among us have far less of the faults which I am about to indicate than any others I have ever attended. But still, they have some of the faults, and I hope that what we shall say will be taken personally home by every brother who is in the habit of engaging publicly in supplication at prayer meetings. Is it not a fact, that as soon as you enter the meeting, you feel that if you are called upon to pray, you have to exercise a gift? And that gift, in the case of many praying men (to speak harshly, perhaps, but I think honestly) lies in having a good memory to remember a great many texts which always have been quoted since the days of our grandfather's grandfather, and to be able to repeat them in good regular order. The gift lies also in some churches, especially in village churches, in having strong lungs so as to be able to hold out, without taking a breath for 25 minutes when you are brief, and three quarters of an hour when you are rather drawn out! The gift lies also in being able not to ask for anything in particular, but in passing through a range of everything, making the prayer not an arrow with a point, but rather like a nondescript machine that has no point whatever, and yet is meant to be all point, which is aimed at everything and consequently strikes nothing! Those brothers are often the most frequently asked to pray who have those peculiar, and perhaps, excellent gifts-although I certainly must say that I cannot obey the apostle's injunction in coveting very earnestly such gifts as these! Now, if instead, thereof, some man is asked to pray who has never prayed before in public-suppose he rises and says, "Oh Lord, I feel myself such a sinner that I can scarcely speak to You. Lord, help me to pray! O Lord, save my poor soul! O that You would save my old companions! Lord, bless our minister! Be pleased to give us a revival. O Lord, I can say no more; hear me for Jesus' sake! Amen." Well then, you feel somehow as if you had begun to pray yourself! You feel an interest in that man partly from fear lest he should stop, and also because you are sure that what he did say, he meant. And if another should get up after that, and pray in the same spirit, you go out and say, "This is real prayer." I would sooner have three minutes of prayer like that, than 30 minutes of the other sort, because the one is praying, and the other is preaching! Allow me to quote what an old preacher said upon the subject of prayer, and give it to you as a little word of advice- "Remember, the Lord will not hear you because of the arithmetic of your prayers-He does not count their numbers. He will not hear you because of the rhetoric of your prayers-He does not care for the eloquent language in which they are conveyed. He will not listen to you because of the geometry of your prayers-He does not compute them by their length, or by their breadth. He will not regard you because of the music of your prayers-He does not care for sweet voices, or for harmonious periods. Neither will He look at you because of the logic of your prayers-because they are well arranged and excellently compartmented. But He will hear you and He will measure the amount of the blessing He will give you according to the divinity of your prayers! If you can plead the person of Christ, and if the Holy Spirit inspires you with zeal and earnestness-the blessings which you shall ask shall surely come to you." Brethren, I would like to burn the whole stock of old prayers that we have been using this 50 years; That "oil that goes from vessel to vessel;" that "horse that rushes into the battle"; that misquoted mangled text, "Where two or three are met together, You will be in the midst of them and that to bless them"- and all those other quotations which we have been manufacturing, and dislocating, and copying from man to man! I would we came to speak to God, just out of our own head! It would be a grand thing for our prayer meetings-they would be better attended-and I am sure they would be more fruitful if every man would shake off that habit of formality and talk to God as a child talks to his father-ask Him for what we need, and then sit down and have done!

I say this with all Christian earnestness. Often, because I have not chosen to pray in any conventional form, people have said, "That man is not reverent!" My dear sir, you are not a judge of my reverence! To my own Master, I stand or fall. I do not think that Job quoted anybody; I do not think that Jacob quoted the old saint in heaven-his father, Abraham. I do not find Jesus Christ quoted Scripture in prayer. They did not pray in other people's words, but they prayed in their own. God does not need you to go gathering up those excellent but very musty spices of the old sanctuary; He wants the new oil just distilled from the fresh olive of your own soul! He wants spices and frankincense, not of the old chests, where they have been lying until they have lost their savor, but He wants fresh incense and fresh myrrh, brought from the Ophir of your own soul's experience! Look well to it that you really pray-do not learn the language of prayer-seek the spirit of prayer, and God Almighty will bless you and make you mightier in your supplications.

I have said, "Look about you." I want you to continue the work and look about at your own closets. Oh, brothers and sisters, there is no place that some of us need to be so much ashamed to look at, as our closet door! I cannot say the hinges are rusty; they do open and shut at their appointed seasons. I cannot say that the door is locked and cobwebbed; we do not neglect prayer itself, but those walls, those beams out of the wall, what a tale might they tell! "Oh," the wall might cry out, "I have heard you when you have been in so much a hurry that you could scarcely spend two minutes with your God! And I have heard you, too, when you were neither asleep nor awake, and when you did not know what you were saying." Then one beam might cry out, "I have heard you come and spend 10 minutes and not ask for anything-at least your heart did not ask-the lips moved but the heart was silent." How might another beam cry out-"Oh, I have heard you groan out your soul, but I have seen you go away distrustful, not believing your prayer was heard, quoting the promise but not thinking God would fulfill it." Surely the four walls of the closet might come together and fall down upon us in their anger, because we have so often insulted God with our unbelief, and with our hurry and with all manner of sins. We have insulted Him even at His mercy seat-on the spot where His condescension is most fully manifested! Is it not so with you? Must we not each confess it in our turn? See to it then, Christian brothers and sisters that an amendment be made, and may God make you mightier, and more successful in your prayers than up to now!

III. But not to detain you, the last point is, look upward, LOOK ABOVE. Look above, Christian brothers and sisters, and let us weep. Oh God, You have given us a mighty weapon, and we have permitted it to rust! You have given us that which is mighty as Yourself, and we have let that power lie dormant! Would it not be a vile crime if a man had an eye given him which he would not open, or a hand that he would not lift up, or a foot that grew stiff because he would not use it? And what must we say of ourselves when God has given us power in prayer, matchless power, and full of blessedness to ourselves and of unnumbered mercies to others, and yet that power lies still? Oh, if the universe were as still as we are, where should we be? Oh God, You give light to the sun, and it shines with it! You give light even to the stars and they twinkle; to the winds You give force and they blow; and to the air You give life and it moves and men breathe thereof! But to Your people You have given a gift that is better than force, and life, and light-and yet they permit it to lie still- almost forgetful that they wield the power, seldom exercising it, though it would be blessed to countless myriads! Weep, Christian! Constantine, the Emperor of Rome, saw that on the coins of the other Emperors, their images were in an erect posture-triumphing. Instead, thereof, he ordered that his image should be struck kneeling, for said he-"That is the way in which I have triumphed." We shall never triumph till our image is struck kneeling! The reason why we have been defeated, and why our banners trail in the dust is because we have not prayed. Go-go back to your God with sorrow-confess before Him, children of Ephraim, that you were armed and carried bows, but turned your backs in the day of battle! Go to your God and tell Him that if souls are not saved, it is not because He has not power to save, but because you have never travailed, as it were, in birth for perishing sinners! Your hearts have not sounded like a harp for Kirharesh, neither has your spirit been moved because of the defenses of the tribe of Reuben. Wake up, wake up, you people of Israel; be astonished, you careless ones-you who have neglected prayer. You sinners who are Zion's own, and who have been at ease, wake yourselves up! Wrestle and strive with your God, and then the blessing shall come-the early and the latter rain of His mercy-and the earth shall bring forth plenteously, and all the nations shall call Him blessed! Look up then, and weep.

Once more, look up and rejoice. Though you have sinned against Him, He loves you still! You have not prayed unto Him, nor sought His face, but behold He cries to you still-"Seek My face." And He says not, "Seek Me in vain." You may not have gone to the fountain, but it flows as freely as before. You have shut your eyes to that sun, but it still shines upon you with all of its luster. You have not drawn near to God, but He waits to be still gracious, and is ready to hear all your petitions! Behold, He says to you, "Inquire of Me concerning things to come, and concerning My sons and daughters. Command Me!" What a blessed thing it is that the Master in heaven is always ready to hear! Augustine has a very beautiful thought upon the parable of the man who knocked at his friend's door at midnight, saying, "Friend, give me three loaves." His paraphrase of it runs something like this-"I knock at mercy's door, and it is the dead of night; will not some of the servants of the house come and answer me? No, I knock, but they are asleep. Oh, you apostles of God-you glorified martyrs-you are asleep, you rest in your beds, you cannot hear my prayer! But will not the children answer? Are there not children who are ready to come and open the door to their brother? No. They are asleep. My brethren who have departed-with whom I took sweet counsel, and who were the companions of my heart-you cannot answer me for you rest in Jesus. Your works do follow you, but you cannot work for me. But while the servants are asleep, and while the children cannot answer, the Master is awake-awake at midnight, too! It may be midnight with my soul, but He hears me, and when I am saying, 'Give me three loaves,' He comes to the door and gives me as much as I need." Christian, look up, then, and rejoice! There is always an open ear if you have an open mouth! There is always a ready hand if you have a ready heart! You have but to cry, and the Lord hears! No, before you call He will answer and while you are speaking He will hear! Oh, be not backward, then, in prayer! Go to Him when you reach your home. No, on the very way, lift up your hearts silently, and whatever your petition or request may be, ask it in Jesus' name, and it shall be done unto you.

Yet, again, look up, dear Christian brothers and sisters, and amend your prayers from this time forth. Look on prayer no longer as a romantic fiction or as an arduous duty. Look at it as a real power-as a real pleasure. When philosophers discover some latent power, they seem to have a delight to put it in action. I believe there have been many great engineers who have designed and constructed some of the most wonderful of human works-not because they would be remunerated, but simply from a love of showing their own power to accomplish wonders-to show the world what skill could do, and what man could accomplish, they have tempted companies into speculations that could never remunerate, as far as I could see, in order that they might have an opportunity of displaying their genius. O Christians-shall a great engineer attempt great works, and display his power, and will you who have a mightier power than ever was wielded by any man apart from his God-will you let that be still? No, think of some great objective and strain the sinews of your supplication for it! Let every vein of your heart be full to the brim with the rich blood of desire-and struggle and wrestle and tug and strive with God for it, using the promises and pleading the attributes-and see if God does not give you your heart's desire. I challenge you this day to exceed in prayer my Master's bounty! I throw down the gauntlet to you! Believe Him to be more than He is! Open your mouth so wide that He cannot fill it! Go to Him now for more faith than the promise warrants-venture it, risk it, outdo the Eternal if it is possible! Attempt it, or as I would rather put it thus, take your petitions and needs and see if He does not honor you. Try whether if you believe Him He does not fulfill the promise and richly bless you with the anointing oil of His Spirit by which you will be strong in prayer!

I cannot refrain from adding just these few syllables as you go away. I know there are some of you who never prayed in your lives. You have said a form of prayer, perhaps, many years, but have never prayed once. Ah, poor soul, you must be born-again, and until you are born-again you cannot pray as I have been directing the Christian to pray. But let me say this much to you. Does your heart long after salvation? Has the Spirit whispered, "Come to Jesus, sinner, He will hear you"? Believe that whisper, for He will hear you! The prayer of the awakened sinner is acceptable to God. He hears the broken in heart and heals them, too. Take your groans and your sighs to God and He will answer you. "Ah but," says one, "I have nothing to plead." Well but plead as David did-"Pardon my iniquity, for it is great." You have that plea-your iniquity is very great! Then plead that precious blood-that all prevailing plea-say, "For His dear sake who shed His blood," and you shall prevail, sinner! But do not go to God and ask for mercy with your sin in your hands-what would you think of the rebel who appeared before the face of his sovereign, and asked for pardon with the dagger sticking in his belt and with the declaration of his rebellion on his breast? Would he deserve to be pardoned? He could not deserve it in any case, and surely he would deserve double his doom for having thus mocked his master while he pretended to be seeking mercy! If a wife had forsaken her husband, do you think she would have the impudence, with brazen forehead, to come back and ask his pardon leaning on the arm of her lover? No, she could not have such impudence, and yet it is so with you-perhaps asking for mercy and going on in sin-praying to be reconciled to God, and yet harboring and indulging your lusts! Awake! Awake! And call upon your God, sinner! The boat is nearing the rock-perhaps tomorrow it may strike and be shattered and you will be cast into the unfathomable depths of everlasting woe! I say call on your God; and when you call upon Him, cast away your sin or He will not hear you. If you lift up your unholy hands with a lie in your right hand, a prayer is worthless on your lips! Oh, come unto Him, say unto Him, "Take away all iniquity; receive us graciously; love us freely," and He will hear you, and you shall yet pray as prevailing princes and one day shall stand as more than conquerors before the starry throne of Him who ever reigns God over all, blessed forevermore! Amen.

Chapter 2
THE SECRET OF POWER IN PRAYER

"If you abide in Me, and My words abide in you, you shall ask what you
will, and it shall be done unto you."
John 15:7.

The gifts of grace are not enjoyed all at once by believers. Coming unto Christ, we are saved by a true union with Him, but it is by abiding in that union that we further receive the purity, the joy, the power, the blessedness, which are stored up in Him for His people. See how our Lord states this when He speaks to the believing Jews in the eighth chapter of this gospel, at the thirty-first and thirty-second verses-"Then said Jesus to those Jews which believed on Him, If you continue in My word, then are you My disciples indeed; and you shall know the truth, and the truth shall make you free." We do not know all the truth at once; we learn it by abiding in Jesus. Perseverance in grace is an educational process by which we learn the truth fully. The emancipating power of that truth is also gradually perceived and enjoyed. "The truth shall make you free." One bond after another snaps, and we are free indeed. You that are young beginners in the divine life may be cheered to know that there is something better still for you; you have not yet received the full recompense of your faith. As your hymn puts it-"It is better on before." You shall have happier views of heavenly things as you climb the hill of spiritual experience. As you abide in Christ you shall have firmer confidence, richer joy, greater stability, more communion with Jesus, and greater delight in the Lord your God. Infancy is beset with many evils from which manhood is exempt; it is the same in the spiritual as in the natural world.

There are these degrees of attainment among believers, and the Savior here incites us to reach a high position by mentioning a certain privilege which is not for all who say that they are in Christ, but for those only who are abiders in Him. Every believer should be an abider, but many have hardly earned the name as yet. Jesus says, "If you abide in Me, and My words abide in you,

you shall ask what you will, and it shall be done unto you." You have to live with Christ to know Him, and the longer you live with Him the more will you admire and adore Him; yes, and the more you will receive from Him, even grace for grace. Truly He is a blessed Christ to one who is but a month old in grace, but these babes can hardly tell what a precious Jesus He is to those whose acquaintance with Him covers well-near half a century! Jesus, in the esteem of abiding believers, grows sweeter and dearer, fairer and more lovely, day by day. Not that He improves in Himself, for He is perfect, but that as we increase in our knowledge of Him, we appreciate more thoroughly His matchless excellencies. How glowingly do His old acquaintances exclaim, "Yes, He is altogether lovely"! Oh, that we may continue to grow up in Him in all things who is our head, that we thus may prize Him more and more!

I call your earnest attention to our text, begging you to consider with me three questions. First, what is this special blessing? "You shall ask what you will, and it shall be done unto you." Secondly, how is this special blessing obtained? "If you abide in Me, and My words abide in you." Then, thirdly, why is it obtained in this way? There must be a reason for the conditions laid down as needful to obtaining the promised power in prayer. Oh, that the anointing of the Holy Spirit which abides on us may now make this subject very profitable to us!

I. WHAT IS THIS SPECIAL BLESSING? Let us read the verse again. Jesus says, "If you abide in Me, and My words abide in you, you shall ask what you will, and it shall be done unto you."

Observe that our Lord had been warning us that severed from Him, we can do nothing, and Therefore, we might naturally have expected that He would now show us how we can do all spiritual acts. But the text does not run as we should have expected it to run. The Lord Jesus does not say, "Without Me you can do nothing, but if you abide in Me, and My words abide in you, you shall do all spiritual and gracious things." He does not now speak of what they should themselves be enabled to do, but of what should be done unto them, "it shall be done unto you." He says not, "Strength shall be given you sufficient for all those holy doings of which you are incapable apart from Me." That would have been true enough, and it is the truth which we looked for here, but our most wise Lord improves upon all parallelisms of speech, and improves upon all expectancies of heart, and says something better still.

He does not say, "If you abide in Me, and My words abide in you, you shall do spiritual things," but, "you shall ask." By prayer you shall be enabled to do, but before all attempts to do, "You shall ask." The choice privilege here given is a mighty prevailing prayerfulness. Power in prayer is very much the gauge of our spiritual condition, and when that is secured to us in a high degree, we are favored as to all other matters.

One of the first results, then, of our abiding union with Christ will be the certain exercise of prayer, "You shall ask." If others neither seek, nor knock, nor ask, you, at any rate, shall do so. Those who keep away from Jesus do not pray. Those in whom communion with Christ is suspended feel as if they could not pray, but Jesus says, "If you abide in Me, and My words abide in you, you shall ask." Prayer comes spontaneously from those who abide in Jesus, even as certain oriental trees, without pressure, shed their fragrant gums. Prayer is the natural out-gushing of a soul in communion with Jesus. Just as the leaf and the fruit will, come out of the vine-branch without any conscious effort on the part of the branch, but simply because of its living union with the stem, so prayer buds, and blossoms, and fruits, out of souls abiding in Jesus. As stars shine, so do abiders pray. It is their use and their second nature. They do not say to themselves, "Now it is the time for us to get to our task and pray." No, they pray as wise men eat, namely, when the desire for it is upon them. They do not cry out as under bondage, "At this time I ought to be in prayer, but I do not feel like it. What a weariness it is!" but they have a glad errand at the mercy seat, and they are rejoiced to go upon it. Hearts abiding in Christ send forth supplications as fires send out flames and sparks. Souls abiding in Jesus open the day with prayer; prayer surrounds them as an atmosphere all day long; at night they fall asleep praying. I have known them even dream a prayer, and, at any rate, they are able joyfully to say, "When I awake, I am still with You." Habitual asking comes out of abiding in Christ. You will not need urging to prayer when you are abiding with Jesus; He says, "You shall ask," and depend upon it, you will.

You shall also feel most powerfully the necessity of prayer. Your great need of prayer will be vividly seen. Do I hear you say-"What! When we abide in Christ, and His words abide in us, have we not already attained?" Far are we, then, from being satisfied with ourselves, it is then that we feel more than ever that we must ask for more grace. He that, knows Christ best, knows his own necessities best. He that is most conscious of life in Christ is also most convinced of his own death apart from Christ. He who most clearly discerns the perfect character of Jesus, will be most urgent in prayer for grace to grow like Him. The more I see to be in my Lord, the more I desire to obtain from Him, since I know that all that is in Him is put there on purpose that I may receive it. "Of His fullness have all we received, and grace for grace." It is just in proportion as we are linked to Christ's fullness that we feel the necessity of drawing from it by constant prayer. Nobody needs to prove to an abider in Christ the doctrine of prayer, for we enjoy the thing itself. Prayer is now as much a necessity of our spiritual life as breath is of our natural life; we cannot live without asking favors of the Lord. "If you abide in Me, and My words abide in you, you shall ask," and you shall not wish to cease from asking. He has said, "Seek you My face," and your heart will answer, "Your face, Lord, will I seek."

Note next, that the fruit of our abiding is not only the exercise of prayer, and a sense of the necessity of prayer, but it includes liberty in prayer, "You shall ask what you will." Have you not been on your knees at times without power to pray? Have you not felt that you could not plead as you desired? You wanted to pray, but the waters were frozen up, and would not flow. You said mournfully, "I am shut up, and cannot come forth." The will was present, but not the freedom to present that will in prayer. Do you, then, desire liberty in prayer, so that you may speak with God as a man speaks with his friend? Here is the way to it, "If you abide in Me, and My words abide in you, you shall ask what you will." I do not mean that you will gain liberty as to mere fluency of utterance, for that is a very inferior gift. Fluency is a questionable endowment, especially when it is not attended with weight of thought and depth of feeling. Some brethren pray by the yard, but true prayer is measured by weight, and not by length. A single groan before God may have more fullness of prayer in it than a fine oration of great length. He that dwells with God in Christ Jesus, he is the man whose steps are enlarged in intercession. He comes boldly because he abides at the throne. He sees the golden scepter stretched out, and hears the King saying, "Ask what you will and it shall be done unto you." It is the man who abides in conscious union with his Lord who has freedom of access in prayer. Well may he come to Christ readily, for he is in Christ, and abides in Him. Attempt not to seize this holy liberty by excitement, or presumption; there is but one way of really gaining it, and here it is-"If you abide in Me, and My words abide in you, you shall ask what you will." By this means alone shall you be enabled to open your mouth wide, that God may fill it. Thus shall you become Israels, and as princes have power with God.

This is not all; the favored man has the privilege of successful prayer. "You shall ask what you will and it shall be done unto you." You may not do it, but it shall be done unto you. You long to bear fruit; ask, and it shall be done unto you. Look at the vine branch. It simply remains in the vine, and by remaining in the vine the fruit comes from it; it is done unto it. Brother in Christ, the purport of your being, its one object and design, is to bring forth fruit to the glory of the Father; to gain this end you must abide in Christ, as the branch abides in the vine. This is the method by which your prayer for fruitfulness will become successful, "It shall be done unto you." Concerning this matter, "you shall ask what you will and it shall be done unto you." You shall have wonderful prevalence with God in prayer, insomuch that before you call He will answer, and while you are yet speaking He will hear. "The desire of the righteous shall be granted." To the same effect is the other text, "Delight yourself also in the Lord; and He shall give you the desires of your heart." There is a great breadth in this text, "You shall ask what you will and it shall be done unto you." The Lord gives the abider carte blanche. He puts into his hand a signed check, and permits him to fill it up as he wills.

Does the text mean what it says? I never knew my Lord to say anything He did not mean. I am sure that He may sometimes mean more than we understand Him to say, but He never means less. Mind you, He does not say to all men, "I will give you whatever you ask." Oh no, that would be an unkind kindness, but He speaks to His disciples, and says, "If you abide in Me, and My words abide in you, you shall ask what you will and it shall be done unto you." It is to a certain class of men who have already received great grace at His hands-it is to them He commits this marvelous power of prayer. O my dear friends, if I may covet earnestly one thing above every other, it is this; that I may be able to ask what I will of the Lord, and have it. The prevailer in prayer is the man to preach successfully, for he may well prevail with man for God when he has already prevailed with God for men. This is the man to face the difficulties of business life, for what can baffle him when he can take all to God in prayer? One such man as this, or one such woman as this in a church, is worth ten thousand of us common people. In these we find the peerage of the skies. In these are the men in who is fulfilled God's purpose concerning man, whom He made to have dominion over all the works of His hands. The stamp of sovereignty is on the brows of these men; they shape the history of nations, they guide the current events through their power on high. We see Jesus with all things put under Him by the divine purpose, and as we rise into that image, we also are clothed with dominion, and are made kings and priests unto God. Behold Elijah, with the keys of the rain swinging at his girdle; he shuts or opens the windows of heaven! There are such men still alive. Aspire to be such men and women, I beseech you, that to you, the text may be fulfilled, "You shall ask what you will and it shall be done unto you."

The text seems to imply that, if we reach this point of privilege, this gift shall be perpetuity, "You shall ask," you shall always ask; you shall never get beyond asking, but you shall ask successfully, for "You shall ask what you will, and it shall be done unto you." Here we have the gift of continual prayer. Not for the week of prayer, not during a month's conference, nor upon a few special occasions shall you pray prevailingly, but you shall possess this power with God so long as you abide in Christ, and His words abide in you. God will put His omnipotence at your disposal; He will put forth His Godhead to fulfill the desires which His own Spirit has worked in you. I wish I could make this jewel glitter before the eyes of all the saints till they cried out, "Oh that we had it!" This power in prayer is like the sword of Goliath; wisely may every David say-"There is none like it; give it to me." This weapon of all-prayer beats the enemy, and, at the same time, enriches its possessor with all the wealth of God. How can he lack anything to whom the Lord has said, "Ask what you will and it shall be done unto you"? Oh, come, let us seek this gift. Listen, and learn the way. Follow me, while by the light of the text I point out the path. May the Lord lead us in it by His Holy Spirit!

II. The privilege of mighty prayerfulness- HOW IS IT TO BE OBTAINED? The answer is, "If you abide in Me, and My words abide in you." Here are the two feet by which we climb to power with God in prayer.

Beloved, the first line tells us that we are to abide in Christ Jesus our Lord. It is taken for granted that we are already in Him. May it be taken for granted in your case, dear hearer? If so, you are to abide where you are. As believers we are to remain tenaciously clinging to Jesus, lovingly knit to Jesus. We are to abide in Him, by always trusting Him and Him only, with the same simple faith which joined us to Him at the first. We must never admit any other thing or person into our heart's confidence as our hope of salvation, but rest alone in Jesus as we received Him at the first. His Godhead, His manhood, His life, His death, His resurrection, His glory at the right hand of the Father- in a word, Himself must be our heart's sole reliance. This is absolutely essential. A temporary faith will not save; an abiding faith is needful.

But abiding in the Lord Jesus does not only mean trusting in Him; it includes our yielding ourselves up to Him to receive His life, and to let that life work out its results in us. We live in Him, by Him, for Him, to Him, when we abide in Him. We feel that all our separate life has gone; for "you are dead, and your life is hid with Christ." We are nothing if we get away from Jesus; we would then be branches withered, and fit only to be cast into the fire. We have no reason for existence except that which we find in Christ, and what a marvelous reason that is! The vine needs the branch as truly as the branch needs the vine. No vine ever bore any fruit except upon its branches. Truly it bears all the branches, and so bears all the fruit; but yet it is by the branch that the vine displays its fruitfulness. Thus are abiding believers needful to the fulfillment of their Lord's design. Wonderful thing to say, but the saints are needful to their Savior! The church is His body; the fullness of Him that fills all in all. I want you to recognize this, that you may see your blessed responsibility, your practical obligation to bring forth fruit, that the Lord Jesus may be glorified in you. Abide in Him. Never remove from your consecration to His honor and glory. Never dream of being your own master. Be not the servant of men, but abide in Christ. Let Him be the object, as well as the source, of your existence. Oh, if you get there, and stop there in perpetual communion with your Lord, you will soon realize a joy, a delight, a power in prayer, such as you never knew before. There are times when we are conscious that we are in Christ, and we know our fellowship with Him, and oh, the joy and the peace which we drink from this cup! Let us abide there. "Abide in Me," says Jesus. You are not to come and go, but to abide. Let that blessed sinking of yourself into His life, the spending of all your powers for Jesus, and the firm faith of your union with Him remain in you forever. Oh, that we might attain to this by the Holy Spirit!

As if to help us to understand this, our gracious Lord has given us a delightful parable. Let us look through this discourse of the vine and its branches. Jesus says, "Every branch in Me that bears fruit, He purges it." Take care that you abide in Christ when you are being purged. "Oh," says one, "I thought I was a Christian; but, alas! I have more troubles than ever, men ridicule me, the devil tempts me, and my business affairs go wrong."

Brother, if you are to have power in prayer you must take care that you abide in Christ when the sharp knife is cutting everything away. Endure trial, and never dream of giving up your faith because of it. Say, "Though He slay me, yet will I trust in Him." Your Lord warned you when you first came into the vine that you would have to be purged and cut closely, and if you are now feeling the purging process, you must not think that some strange thing has happened unto you. Rebel not because of anything you may have to suffer from the dear hand of your heavenly Father, who is the husbandman of the vineyard. No, but cling to Jesus all the more closely. Say, "Cut, Lord, cut to the quick if You will, but I will cling to You. To whom should we go? You have the words of eternal life." Yes, cling to Jesus when the purging knife is in His hand, and so "shall you ask what you will, and it shall be done unto you."

Take care, also, that when the purging operation has been carried out you still cleave to your Lord. Notice the third verse, "Now you are clean through the word which I have spoken unto you. Abide in Me, and I in you." Abide after cleansing where you were before cleansing. When you are sanctified, abide where you were when first justified. When you see the work of the Spirit increasing in you, do not let the devil tempt you to boast that now you are somebody, and need not come to Jesus as a poor sinner, and rest in His precious blood alone for salvation. Abide still in Jesus. As you kept to Him when the knife cut you, keep to Him now that the tender grapes begin to form. Do not say to yourself, "What a fruitful branch I am! How greatly I adorn the vine! Now I am full of vigor!" You are nothing and nobody. Only as you abide in Christ are you one whit better than the waste wood which is burned in the fire. "But do we not make progress?" Yes, we grow, but we abide; we never go an inch further, we abide in Him; or, if not, we are cast forth, and are withered. Our whole hope lies in Jesus at our best times as well as at our worst. Jesus says, "Now you are clean through the word which I have spoken unto you. Abide in Me, and I in you."

Abide in Him as to all your fruitfulness. "As the branch cannot bear fruit of itself except it abide in the vine, no more can you, except you abide in Me." "Here, then, I have something to do," cries one. Certainly you have, but not apart from Jesus. The branch has to bear fruit, but if the branch imagines that it is going to produce a cluster, or even a grape, out of itself alone, it is utterly mistaken. The fruit of the branch must come forth of the stem. Your work for Christ must be Christ's work in you, or else it will be good for nothing. I pray you, see to this. Your Sunday school teaching, your preaching, or whatever you do, must be done in Christ Jesus. Not by your natural talent can you win souls, nor by plans of your own inventing can you save men. Beware of homemade schemes. Do for Jesus what Jesus bids you do. Remember that our work for Christ, as we call it, must be Christ's work first, if it is to be accepted of Him. Abide in Him as to your fruit-bearing.

Yes, abide in Him as to your very life. Do not say, "I have been a Christian man now twenty or thirty years, I can do without continued dependence upon Christ." No, you could not do without Him if you were as old as Methuselah. Your very being as a Christian depends upon your still clinging, still trusting, still depending, and this He must give you, for it all comes from Him, and Him alone. To sum it all up, if you want that splendid power in prayer of which I spoke just now, you must remain in loving, living, lasting, conscious, practical, abiding union with the Lord Jesus Christ, and if you get to that by divine grace, then you shall ask what you will, and it shall be done unto you.

But there is a second qualification mentioned in the text, and you must not forget it-"and My words abide in you." How important, then, are Christ's words! He said in the fourth verse, "Abide in Me, and I in you," and now as a parallel to this it is, "If you abide in Me, and My words abide in you." What, then, are Christ's words and Himself identical? Yes, practically so. Some talk about Christ being the Master, but as to doctrine, they do not care what His word declares. So long as their hearts are right towards His person they claim liberty of thought. Yes, but this is a mere subterfuge. We cannot separate Christ from the Word, for in the first place, He is the Word, and, in the next place, how dare we call Him Master and Lord and do not the things which He says, and reject the truth which He teaches? We must obey His precepts or He will not accept us as disciples. Especially that precept of love which is the essence of all His words. We must love God and our brethren; yes, we must cherish love to all men, and seek their good. Anger and malice must be far from us. We must walk even as He walked. If Christ's words abide not in you, both as to belief and practice, you are not in Christ. Christ and His gospel and His commands are one. If you will not have Christ and His words, neither will He have you nor your words, but you shall ask in vain, you shall by and by give up asking, you shall become as a withered branch. Beloved, I am persuaded better things of you, and things that accompany salvation, though I thus speak.

Oh for grace to pass through these two-leaved gates, these two golden doors! "If you abide in Me, and My words abide in you." Push through the two and enter into this large room-"You shall ask what you will and it shall be done unto you."

III. It is my last work to try to show WHY THIS PRIVILEGE SHOULD BE SO OBTAINED. This extraordinary power of prayer, why is it given to those who abide in Christ? May what I have to say encourage you to make the glorious attempt to win this pearl of great price! Why is it, that by abiding in Christ, and having His words abide in us, we get to this liberty and prevalence in prayer?

I answer, first, because of the fullness of Christ. You may very well ask what you will when you abide in Christ, because whatever you may require is already lodged in Him. Good Bishop Hall worked out this thought in a famous passage. I will give you the substance of it. Do you desire the grace of the Spirit? Go to your Lord's anointing. Do you seek holiness? Go to His example. Do you desire pardon of sin? Look to His blood. Do you need mortification of sin? Look to His crucifixion. Do you need to be buried to the world? Go to His tomb. Do you want to feel the fullness of a heavenly life? Behold His resurrection. Would you rise above the world? Mark His ascension. Would you contemplate heavenly things? Remember His session at the right hand of God, and know that He "has raised us up together, and made us sit together in heavenly places." I see clearly enough why the branch gets all it wants while it abides in the stem, since all it wants is already in the stem, and is placed there for the sake of the branch. What does the branch want more than the stem can give it? If it did want more it could not get it, for it has no other means of living but by sucking its life out of the stem. O my precious Lord, if I want anything which is not in You, I desire always to be without it. I desire to be denied a wish which wanders outside of Yourself. But if the supply of my desire is already in You for me, why should I go elsewhere? You are my all; where else should I look? Beloved, "it pleased the Father that in Him should all fullness dwell," and the good pleasure of the Father is our good pleasure also; we are glad to draw everything from Jesus. We feel sure that, ask what we will, we shall have it, since He has it ready for us.

The next reason for this is, the richness of the Word of God. Catch this thought, "If My words abide in you, you shall ask what you will and it shall be done unto you." The best praying man is the man who is most believingly familiar with the promises of God. After all, prayer is nothing but taking God's promises to Him, and saying to Him, "Do as You have said." Prayer is the promise utilized. A prayer which is not based on a promise has no true foundation. If I go to the bank without a check I need not expect to get money; it is the "order to pay" which is my power inside the bank, and my warrant for expecting to receive. You that have Christ's words abiding in you are equipped with those things which the Lord regards with attention. If the Word of God abides in you, you are the man that can pray, because you meet the great God with His own words, and thus overcome omnipotence with omnipotence. You put your finger down upon the very lines, and say, "Do as You have said." This is the best praying in all the world. O Beloved, be filled with God's Word. Study what Jesus has said, what the Holy Spirit has left on record in this divinely-inspired Book, and in proportion as you feed on the Word, and are filled with the Word, and retain the Word in your faith, and obey the Word in your life-in that proportion you will be a master-man in the art of prayer. You have acquired skill as a wrestler with the covenant angel in proportion as you can plead the promises of your faithful God. Be well instructed in the doctrines of grace, and let the word of Christ dwell in you richly, that you may know how to prevail at the throne of grace. Abiding in Christ and His words abiding in you, are like the right hand and the left hand of Moses, which were held up in prayer, so that Amalek was smitten, Israel was delivered, and God was glorified.

Let us go a little further; you still may say you do not quite see why a man who abides in Christ, and in whom Christ's words abide, should be allowed to ask whatever he wills, and it shall be done unto him. I answer you again; it is so, because in such a man as that there is a predominance of grace which causes him to have a renewed will, which is according to the will of God. Suppose a man of God is in prayer, and he thinks that such and such a thing is desirable, yet he remembers that he is nothing but a babe in the presence of his all-wise Father, and so he bows his will, and asks as a favor to be taught what to will. Though God bids him ask what he wills, he shrinks and cries, "My Lord, here is a request which I am not quite clear about. As far as I can judge, it is a desirable thing, and I will it, but, Lord, I am not fit to judge for myself, and therefore I pray You, give not as I will, but as You will." Do you not see that when we are in such a condition as this, our real will is God's will? Deep down in our hearts we will only that, which the Lord Himself wills, and what is this but to ask what we will, and it is done to us? It becomes safe for God to say to the sanctified soul, "Ask what you will and it shall be done unto you." The heavenly instincts of that man lead him right; the grace that is within his soul thrusts down all covetous lusting and foul desires, and his will is the actual shadow of God's will. The spiritual life is master in him, and so his aspirations are holy, heavenly, God-like. He has been made a partaker of the divine nature, and as a son is like his father, so now in desire and will, he is one with his God. As the echo answers to the voice, so does the renewed heart echo the mind of the Lord. Our desires are reflected beams of the divine will; you shall ask what you will, and it shall be even so.

You clearly see that the holy God cannot pick up a common man in the street, and say to him, "I will give you whatever you will." What would he ask for? He would ask for a good drink, or permission to enjoy himself in evil lust. It would be very unsafe to trust the most of men with this permit. But when the Lord has taken a man, and has made him new, has quickened him into newness of life, and has formed him in the image of His dear Son, then He can trust him! Behold, the great Father treats us in our measure as He treats His First-born. Jesus could say, "I know that You hear Me always," and the Lord is educating us to the selfsame assurance. We can say with one of old, "My God will hear me." Do not your mouths water for this privilege of prevailing prayer? Do not your hearts long to get at this? It is by the way of holiness, it is by the way of union to Christ, it is by the way of a permanent abiding in Him, and an obedient holding fast of His truth, that you are to come to this privilege. Behold the only safe and true way. When once that way is really trodden, it is a most sure and effectual way of gaining substantial power in prayer.

I have not quite done. A man will succeed in prayer when his faith is strong, and this is the case with those who abide in Jesus. It is faith that prevails in prayer. The real eloquence of prayer is a believing desire. "All things are possible to him that believes." A man abiding in Christ with Christ's words abiding in him, is eminently a believer, and consequently eminently successful in prayer. He has strong faith indeed, for his faith has brought him into vital contact with Christ, and he is therefore at the source of every blessing, and may drink to his full at the well itself.

Such a man, once more, will also possess the indwelling of the Spirit of God. If we abide in Christ, and His words abide in us, then the Holy Spirit has come and taken up His residence in us, and what better help in prayer can we have? Is it not a wonderful thing that the Holy Spirit Himself makes intercession in the saints according to the will of God? He "makes intercession for us with groans that cannot be uttered." What man knows the mind of a man save the spirit of a man? The Spirit of God knows the mind of God, and He works in us to will what God wills, so that a believing man's prayer is God's purpose reflected in the soul as in a mirror. The eternal decrees of God project their shadows over the hearts of godly men in the form of prayer. What God intends to do He tells unto His servants by inclining them to ask Him to do what He Himself is resolved to do. God says, "I will do this and that," but then He adds, "For this will I be inquired of by the house of Israel to do it for them." How clear it is that if we abide in Christ, and His words abide in us, we may ask what we will! For we shall only ask what the Spirit of God moves us to ask, and it were impossible that God the Holy Spirit and God the Father should be at cross-purposes with one another. What the one prompts us to ask, the other has assuredly determined to bestow.

I struck out a line just now to which I must return for a single moment. Beloved, do you not know that when we abide in Christ, and His words abide in us, the Father looks upon us with the same eye with which He looks upon His dear Son? Christ is the vine, and the vine includes the branches. The branches are a part of the vine. God, therefore, looks upon us as part of Christ-members of His body, of His flesh, and of His bones. Such is the Father's love to Jesus that He denies Him nothing. He was obedient to death, even the death of the cross; therefore does His Father love Him, as the God-man Mediator, and He will grant Him all His petitions. And is it so, that when you and I are in real union to Christ, the Lord God looks upon us in the same way as He looks on Jesus, and says to us, "I will deny you nothing; you shall ask what you will, and it shall be done unto you"? So do I understand the text.

I call your attention to the fact that in that fifteenth chapter, the ninth verse, which I did not read this morning, runs thus-"As the Father has loved Me, so have I loved you." The same love which God gives to His Son, the Son gives to us, and therefore we are dwellers in the love of the Father and of the Son. How can our prayers be rejected? Will not infinite love have respect unto our petitions? O dear brother in Christ, if your prayers speed not at the throne, suspect that there is some sin that hinders them; your Father's love sees a necessity for chastening you this way. If you do not abide in Christ, how can you hope to pray successfully? If you pick and choose His words, and doubt this, and doubt that, how can you hope to speed to the throne? If you are willfully disobedient to any of His words, will not this account for failure in prayer? But abide in Christ, and take fast hold upon His words, and be altogether His disciple, then shall you be heard of Him. Sitting at Jesus' feet, hearing His words, you may lift up your eyes to His dear face, and say, "My Lord, hear me now," and He will answer you graciously; He will say unto you, "I have heard you in a time accepted, and in the day of salvation have I succored you. Ask what you will, and it shall be done unto you." Oh for power at the mercy seat!

Beloved friends, do not hear this sermon, and then go away and forget it. Try to reach this place of boundless influence. What a church we could be, if you were all mighty in prayer! Dear children of God, do you want to be half starved? Beloved brethren, do you desire to be poor, little, puny, driveling children, who will never grow into men? I pray you, aspire to be strong in the Lord, and to enjoy this exceedingly high privilege. What an army would you be if you all had this power with God in prayer! It is within your reach, you children of God! Only abide in Christ, and let His words abide in you, and then this special privilege will be yours. These are not irksome duties, but they are in themselves a joy. Go in for them with your whole heart, and then you shall get this added to you, that you shall ask what you will, and it shall be done unto you.

Unhappily, to a portion of this congregation my text says nothing at all, for some of you are not even in Christ, and therefore you cannot abide in Him. O sirs, what shall I say to you? You seem to me to miss a very heaven even now. If there were no hell hereafter, it is hell enough not to know Christ now, not to know what it is to prevail with God in prayer, not to know the choice privilege of abiding in Him, and His words abiding in you. Your first matter is that you believe in Jesus Christ to the saving of your souls, yielding your souls to His cleansing, your lives to His government. God has sent Him forth as a Savior, accept Him. Receive Him as your Teacher; yield yourself up to Him as your Master. May His gracious Spirit come and do this work upon you now, and then, after this, but not before, you may aspire to this honor. First of all-"You must be born again." I cannot say to you as you are now, "Grow," because you will only grow a bigger sinner. However much you may be developed, you will only develop what is in you, and that is, the heir of wrath will become more and more the child of evil. You must be made anew in Christ; there must be an absolute change, a reversal of all the currents of nature, a making you a new creature in Christ Jesus, and then you may aspire to abide in Christ, and let His words abide in you, and the consequent prevalence with God in prayer shall be yours.

Gracious Lord, help us this morning. Poor creatures as we are, we can only lie at Your feet. Come Yourself, and uplift us to Yourself, for Your mercy's sake! Amen.

Chapter 3
THE CONDITIONS OF POWER IN PRAYER

"And whatsoever we ask, we receive of Him, because we keep His
commandments, and do those things that are pleasing in His sight. And
this is His commandment, That we should believe on the name of His Son
Jesus Christ, and love one another, as He gave us commandment.
And he that keeps His commandment dwells in Him, and He in him.
And hereby we know that He abides in us, by the Spirit which He has
given us."
1 John 3:22-24.

I thought of addressing you this morning upon the importance of prayer and I designed earnestly to stir you up to pray for me and for the Lord's work in this place. Truly, I do not think I could have had a weightier subject, or one which weighs more upon my soul. If I were only allowed to offer one request to you it would be this-"Brothers and sisters, pray for us." Of what use can our ministry be without the divine blessing and how can we expect the divine blessing unless it is sought for by the Church of God? I would say it even with tears, "Brethren, pray for us:" do not restrain prayer: on the contrary, be abundant in intercession, for so, and so only, can our prosperity as a church be increased, or even continued. But then, the question occurred to me, what if there should be something in the church which would prevent our prayers being successful? That is an important question and one which ought to be considered most earnestly even before we exhort you to intercession. As we have already been taught by the first chapter of Isaiah, the prayers of an unholy people will soon become abominations to God. "When you spread forth your hands, I will hide My eyes from you; yes, when you make many prayers, I will not hear." Churches may fall into such a state that the devotions will be an iniquity. "Even the solemn meeting" will be weariness unto the Lord. There may be evils in the heart of any one of us which may render it impossible for God, in consistency with His own character and attributes, to have any regard to our intercessions. If we regard iniquity in our hearts the Lord will not hear us. According to our text there are some things which are essential to prevalence in prayer. God will hear all true prayer, but there are certain things which the people of God must possess or else their prayers will fall short of the mark. The text tells us, "Whatever we ask we receive of Him, because we keep His commandments, and do those things that are pleasing in His sight." Now, this morning the subject of consideration will be the essentials to power in prayer; what we must do, what we must be, what we must have, if we are to prevail habitually with God in prayer, as a matter of constant fact. Let us learn how to become Elijahs and Jacobs.

I. I shall begin, first, by considering THE ESSENTIALS OF POWER IN PRAYER. We must make a few distinctions at the outset. I take it there is a great difference between the prayer of a soul that is seeking mercy and the prayer of a man who is saved. I would say to every person present, whatever his character, if you sincerely seek mercy of God through Jesus Christ you shall have it. Whatever may have been your previous condition of life, if you now penitently seek Jehovah's face through the appointed Mediator, He will be found of you. If the Holy Spirit has taught you to pray, hesitate no longer but hasten to the cross and there rest your guilty soul on Jesus. I know of no qualifications for the sinner's first prayer except sincerity, but we must speak in a different way to those of you who are saved. You have now become the people of God and while you shall be heard just as the sinner would be heard, and shall daily find the necessary grace which every seeker receives in answer to prayer, yet you are now a child of God and you are under a special discipline peculiar to the regenerated family. In that discipline answers to prayer occupy a high position and are of eminent use. There is something for a believer to enjoy over and above bare salvation. There are mercies, blessings, comforts and favors which render his present life useful, happy and honorable. And these he shall have irrespective of character. They are not vital matters with regard to salvation; those the believer possesses unconditionally, for they are covenant blessings; but we now refer to the honors and the dainties of the house, which are given or withheld according to our obedience as the Lord's children. If you neglect the conditions appended to these, your heavenly Father will withhold them from you. The essential blessings of the covenant of grace stand unconditioned; the invitation to seek for mercy is addressed to those who have no qualifications whatever, except their need. But come inside the divine family as saved men and women and you will find that other choice blessings are given or withheld according to our attention to the Lord's rules in His family. To give a common illustration; if a hungry person were at your door and asked for bread, you would give it to him whatever might be his character. You will also give your child food whatever may be his behavior; you will not deny your child anything that is necessary for life. You will never proceed in any course of discipline against him, so as to deny him his necessary food, or a garment to shield him from the cold; but there are many other things which your child may desire which you will give him if he is obedient, which you will not give if he is rebellious to you. I take it that this illustrates how far the paternal government of God will push this matter and where it will not go.

Understand, also, that the text refers not so much to God's hearing a prayer of His servants now and then, for that He will do, even when His servants are out of course with Him and when He is hiding His face from them. The power in prayer, here intended, is continuous and absolute power with God, so that to quote the words of the text, "Whatever we ask of Him we receive."

For this prayer there are certain prerequisites and essentials, of which we have now to speak, and the first is childlike obedience: "Whatever we ask, we receive of Him, because we keep His commandments." If we are destitute of this the Lord may say to us as He did to His people Israel, "You have forsaken Me, and served other gods, therefore I will deliver you no more. Go and cry unto the gods which you have chosen." Any father will tell you that for him to grant the request of a disobedient child would be to encourage rebellion in the family and render it impossible for him to rule in his own house. It is often incumbent upon the parent to say, "My child, you did not listen to my word just now, and therefore, I cannot listen to yours." Not that the father does not love, but that he does love the child, and because of his love he feels bound to show his displeasure by refusing the request of his erring offspring. God acts with us as we should act towards our refractory children. And if He sees that we will go into sin and transgress, it is a part of His kind paternal discipline to say, "I will shut out your prayer, when you cry unto Me; I will not hear you when you entreat of Me; I will not destroy you, you shall be saved, you shall have the bread of life, and the water of life, but you shall have no more: the luxuries of My kingdom shall be denied you, and anything like special prevalence with Me in prayer you shall not possess." That thus the Lord deals with His own people is clear from the

Eighty-first Psalm: "Oh that My people had hearkened unto Me, and Israel had walked in My ways! I should soon have subdued their enemies, and turned My hand against their adversaries. I should have fed them, also, with the finest of the wheat: and with honey out the rock should I have satisfied you." Why, if the disobedient child of God had the promise put into his hands-"Whatever you ask in prayer, you shall receive," he would be sure to ask for something that would bolster him up in his rebellion. He would be asking for provision for his own lust, and aids for his rebellion. This can never be tolerated. Shall God pander to our corruptions? Shall He find fuel for the flames of carnal passion? A self-willed heart hankers after greater liberty that it may be the more obstinate. A haughty spirit longs for greater elevation that it may be prouder still. A slothful spirit asks for greater ease that it may yet be more indolent; and a domineering spirit asks for more power that it may have more opportunities of oppression. As such the man is, will his prayer be a rebellious spirit offers self-willed and proud prayers. Shall God listen to such prayers as these? It cannot be. He will give us what we ask if we keep His commandments, but if we become disobedient and reject His government He, also, will reject our prayers and say, "If you walk contrary to Me, I also will walk contrary to you: with the forward, I will show Myself forward." Happy shall we be if through divine grace we can say with David, "I will wash my hands in innocence; so will I compass Your altar, O Lord." This will never be perfect innocence, but it will at least be innocence of the love of sin and of willful revolt from God.

Next to this is another essential to victorious prayer, namely, childlike reverence. Notice the next sentence: We receive what we ask, "because we keep His commandments, and do those things that are pleasing in His sight." We do not allow children, when they have a command from their father, to question its propriety or wisdom. Obedience ends where questioning begins. A child's standard of its duty must not become the measure of the father's right to command: good children say, "Father has bid us to do so-and-so, and therefore we will do it, for we delight to please him always." The weightiest reason for a loving child's action is the persuasion that it would please his parents. And the strongest thing that can be said to hold back a gracious child is to prove that such a course of action would displease his parents. It is precisely so with us towards God, who is a perfect parent, and therefore we may, without fear of mistake, always make His pleasure the rule of right, while the rule of wrong may safely remain that which would displease Him.

Suppose any of us should be self-willed and say, "I shall not do what pleases God, I shall do what pleases myself." Then, observe, what would be the nature of our prayers? Our prayers might then be summed up in the request, "Let me have my own way." And can we expect God to consent to that? Are we to be not only lords over God's heritage but over God Himself? Would you have the Almighty resign His throne to place a proud mortal there? If you have a child in your house who has no respect, whatever, for his father, but who says, "I want to have my own way in all things," if he comes to you with a request, will you stoop to him? Will you allow him to dictate to you and forget the honor due you? Will you say, "Yes, my dear child, I recognize your importance, you shall be lord in the house and whatever you ask for you shall have"! What kind of a house would that be? I fear there are some such houses, for there are foolish parents who suffer their children to become their masters and so make a rod for their own backs. But God's house is not ordered so! He will not listen to His self-willed children, unless it is to hear them in anger and to answer them in wrath. Remember how He heard the prayer of Israel for meat, and when the meat was yet in their mouths it became a curse to them? Many persons are chastened by obtaining their own desires, even as backsliders are filled with their own devices. We must have a childlike reverence of God, so that we feel, "Lord, if what I ask for does not please You, neither would it please me; my desires are put into Your hands to be corrected. Strike the pen through every petition that I offer which is not right, and Lord, put in whatever I have omitted even though I might not have desired it had I remembered it. Good Lord, if I ought to have desired it, hear me as if I had desired it. 'Not as I will, but as You will.'" Now I think you can see that this yielding spirit is essential to continual prevalence with God in prayer. The reverse is a sure barrier to eminence in supplication. The Lord will be reverenced by those who are round about Him. They must have an eye to His pleasure in all that they do and all that they ask, or He will not look upon them with favor.

In the third place, the text suggests the necessity of childlike trust: "And this is His commandment that we should believe on the name of His Son Jesus Christ." Everywhere in Scripture faith in God is spoken of as necessary to successful prayer. We must believe that God is and that He is the rewarder of them that diligently seek Him, or else we have not prayed at all. In proportion to our faith will be the success of our prayer. It is a standing rule of the kingdom, "According to your faith, so be it unto you." Remember how the Holy Spirit speaks by the mouth of the Apostle James, "If any of you lack wisdom, let him ask of God, that gives to all men liberally, and upbraids not; and it shall be given him. But let him ask in faith, nothing wavering; for he that wavers is like a wave of the sea driven with the wind and tossed; for let not that man think that he shall receive anything of the Lord." The text speaks of faith in the name of His Son Jesus Christ, which I understand to mean faith in His declared character, faith in His gospel, faith in the truth concerning His substitution and salvation. Or it may mean faith in the authority of Christ, so that when I plead with God and say, "Do it in the name of Jesus," I mean, "Do for me as You would have done for Jesus, for I am authorized by Him to use His name. Do it for me as You would have done it for Him." He that can pray with faith in the name of Jesus cannot fail, for the Lord Jesus has said, "If you ask anything in My name, I will do it." But there must be faith and if there is no faith we cannot expect to be heard. Do you understand that? Let us come back to our family similitudes again. Suppose a child in the house does not believe his father's word and is constantly saying that he finds his mind full of doubts as to his father's truthfulness? Suppose, indeed, that he tells his brothers and sisters that his faith in his father is very weak? He mentions that wretched fact and is not at all shocked that he should say such a thing, but he rather feels that he ought to be pitied, as if it were an infirmity which he could not avoid. Somehow or other he does not believe that his father speaks the truth and he declares that though he tries to believe his father's promise, yet he cannot. I think a father so basely distrusted would not be in a very great hurry to grant such a son's requests. Indeed, it is very probable that the petitions of the mistrustful son would be such as could not be complied with, even if his father were willing to do so, since they would amount to a gratification of his own unbelief and a dishonor to his parent. For instance, suppose this child should take it into his head to doubt whether his father would provide him with his daily food? He might, then, come to his father and say, "Father, give me enough money to last for the next ten years, for I shall then be a man and shall be able to provide for myself. Give me money down to quiet my fears, for I am in great anxiety." The father replies, "My Son, why should I do that?" And he gets for a reply, "I am very sorry to say it, dear father, but I cannot trust you. I have such a weak faith in you and your love that I am afraid one of these days you will leave me to starve. And therefore I should like to have something sure in the bank." Which of you fathers would listen to a child's request if he sought such a thing? You would feel grieved that thoughts so dishonoring to yourself should pass through the mind of one of your own beloved ones! But you would not and could not, give way to them. Let me, then, ask you to apply the parable to yourselves. Did you never offer requests which were of much the same character? You have been unable to trust God to give you, day by day, your daily bread, and therefore you have been craving for what you call, "some provision for the future." You want a trustier provider than providence, a better security than God's promise. You are unable to trust your heavenly Father's Word. A few bonds of some half-bankrupt foreign government you consider to be far more reliable. You can trust the Sultan of Turkey, or the Viceroy of Egypt, but not the God of the whole earth! In a thousand ways we insult the Lord by imagining "the things which are seen" to be more substantial than His unseen omnipotence. We ask God to give us, at once, what we do not require at present and may never need at all! At bottom, the reason for such desires may be found in a disgraceful distrust of Him which makes us imagine that great stores are necessary to ensure our being provided for. Brethren are you not to blame here, and do you expect the Lord to aid and abet your folly? Shall God pander to your distrust? Shall He give you a heap of cankering gold and silver for thieves to steal and chests of garments to feed moths? Would you have the Lord act as if He admitted the correctness of your suspicions and confessed to unfaithfulness? God forbid! Expect not, therefore, to be heard when your prayer is suggested by an unbelieving heart: "Commit your way unto the Lord; trust also in Him and He shall bring it to pass."

The next essential to continued success in prayer is childlike love: "That we should believe on the name of His Son, Jesus Christ, and love one another as He gave us commandment." The great commandment after faith is love. As it is said of God, "God is Love," so may we say that, "Christianity is love." If we were, each one, incarnations of love we should have attained to the complete likeness of Christ. We should abound in love to God, love to Christ, love to the church, love to sinners and love to men everywhere. When a man has no love to God, he is in the condition of a child without love to his father. Shall his father promise absolutely to fulfill all the desires of his unloving, unfilial heart? Or, if a child has no love to his brothers and sisters, shall the father trust him with an absolute promise, and say, "Ask and it shall be given you?" Why, the unloving son would impoverish the whole family by his selfish demands, regardless of all the rest of the household. He would only care to indulge his own passions. His request would before long be-"Father, give me all the inheritance," or, "Father, regulate the home to suit me and make all my brothers submit to my wishes." Vain of his personal appearance, like Absalom, who was proud of his hair, he would soon seek the kingdom for himself. Few Josephs can wear the garment of many colors and not become household tyrants. Who would allow a prodigal to run off with the estate? Who would be so unwise as to install a greedy, domineering brother in the seat of honor, above his brethren? Therefore, you see that selfishness cannot be trusted with power in prayer. Unloving spirits, that love neither God nor men, cannot be trusted with great, broad, unlimited promises. If God is to hear us we must love God and love our fellow men for, when we love God, we shall not pray for anything that would not honor God and shall not wish to see anything happen to us which would not also bless our brethren. Our hearts will beat true to God and to His creatures and we shall not be wrapped up in ourselves. You must get rid of selfishness before God can trust you with the keys of heaven. When self is dead, then He will enable you to unlock His treasuries and as a prince, shall you have power with God and prevail.

Next to this, we must have childlike ways as well. Read the next verse, "He that keeps His commandments dwells in Him, and He in him." It is one of a child's ways to love its home. The good child, to whose requests its father always listens, loves no place so much as the dear old house where its parents live. Now he who loves and keeps God's commandments is said to dwell in Him-he has made the Lord his dwelling place and abides in holy familiarity with God. In him our Lord's words are fulfilled, "If you abide in Me, and My words abide in you, you shall ask what you will, and it shall be done unto you." Faith and love, like two cherubic wings, have borne up the believer's soul above the world and carried him near to the throne of God. He has become like God and now it is that his prayers are such as God can answer-but until he is thus conformed to the divine mind there must be some limit to the potency of his pleadings. To dwell in God is necessary to power with God. Suppose one of you had a boy, who said, "Father, I do not like my home, I do not care for you and I will not endure the restraints of family rule. I am going to live with strangers, but mark, father, I shall come to you every week and I shall require many things of you. And I shall expect that you will give me whatever I ask from you"? Why, if you are at all fit to be at the head of the house, you will say, "My son, how can you speak to me in such a manner? If you are so self-willed as to leave my house, can you expect that I will do your bidding? If you utterly disregard me, can you expect me to support you in your cruel unkindness and wicked insubordination? No, my son, if you will not remain with me and own me as a father, I cannot promise you anything." And so is it with God. If we will dwell with Him and commune with Him, He will give us all things. If we love Him as He should be loved, and trust Him as He ought to be trusted, then He will hear our requests. But if not, it is not reasonable to expect it. Indeed, it would be a slur upon the divine character for Him to fulfill unholy desires and gratify evil whims. "Delight yourself also in the Lord, and He will give you the desires of your heart," but if you have no delight in God and He is not your dwelling place, He will not answer you. He may give you the bread of affliction and the water of affliction and make life bitter for you, but certainly He will not give you what your heart desires.

One thing more: It appears from the text that we must have a childlike spirit, for, "Hereby we know that He abides in us, by the Spirit which He has given us." What is this but the Spirit of adoption-the Spirit which rules in all the children of God? The willful who think and feel and act differently from God must not expect that God will come round to their way of thinking and feeling and acting. The selfish who are actuated by the spirit of pride, the slothful who are actuated by the love of ease must not expect that God will indulge them. The Holy Spirit, if He rules in us, will subordinate our nature to His own sway and then the prayers which spring out of our renewed hearts will be in keeping with the will of God-and such prayers will naturally be heard. No parent would think of listening to a willful child, to a child that said, "I know my father does not wish me to have this, but I will have it." Why, as a man you would not thus be twisted about by an upstart youngster. Shall God grant us that which we ask for when it is contrary to His holy mind? It must not be! Such a possibility is not conceivable. The same mind must be in us, which is also in Christ Jesus, and then we shall be able to say, "I know that You hear me always."

But we must pass on and occupy your attention, for a few minutes, with another branch of the same subject.

II. In the second place we shall notice THE PREVALENCE OF THESE ESSENTIAL THINGS. If they are in us and abound, our prayers cannot be barren or unprofitable.

First, if we have faith in God, there is no question about God's hearing our prayer. If we can plead, in faith, the name and blood of Jesus, we must obtain answers of peace. But a thousand arguments are suggested. Suppose these prayers concern the laws of nature then the scientific men are against us. What of that? I will glory in giving these scientific men scope enough-I had almost said rope enough. I do not know of any prayer worth praying which does not come into contact with some natural law or other and yet I believe in prayers being heard. It is said that God will not change the laws of nature for us, and I reply, "Whoever said He would!" The Lord has ways of answering our prayers irrespective of the working of miracles or suspending laws. He used to hear prayer by miracle, but as I have often said to you, that seems a rougher way of achieving His purpose; it is like stopping a vast machine for a small result, but He knows how to accomplish His ends and hear our prayers by I know not what secret means. Perhaps there are other forces and laws which He has arranged to bring into action just at times when prayer also acts, for laws just as fixed, and forces just as natural as those which our learned theorizers have been able to discover. The wisest men know not all the laws which govern the universe, no, nor a tenth of them. We believe that the prayers of Christians are a part of the machinery of providence, cogs in the great wheel of destiny, and when God leads His children to pray, He has already set in motion a wheel that is to produce the result prayed for and the prayers offered are moving as a part of the wheel. If there is but faith in God, God must either cease to be, or cease to be true, or else He must hear prayer.

The verse before the text says, "If our heart condemn us not, then have we confidence toward God; and whatever we ask, we receive of Him." He who has a clear conscience comes to God with confidence and that confidence of faith ensures to him the answer of his prayer. Childlike confidence makes us pray as none else can. It makes a man pray for great things which he would never have asked for if he had not learned this confidence. It makes him pray for little things which a great many are afraid to ask for, because they have not yet felt towards God the confidence of children. I have often said that it needs more confidence in God to pray to Him about a little thing than about great things. We fancy that our great things are somewhat worthy of God's regard, though in truth they are little enough to Him! And then we imagine that our little things must be so trifling that it would be almost an insult to bring them before Him, whereas we ought to know that what is very great to a child may be very little to its parent, and yet the parent does not measure the thing from his own point of view but from the child's. You heard your little boy the other day crying bitterly. His mother called him and asked what ailed him? It was a splinter in his finger. Well, that was a small affair. You did not want to call in three surgeons to extract it, or raise a tone and cry in the public press. Bring a needle and we will soon set it right. Oh, but what a great thing it was to that pretty little sufferer as he stood there with eyes all wet with tears of anguish. It was a great concern to him. Now, did it occur to that boy that his pain was too small a thing for his mother to attend to? Not at all! What were mothers and fathers made for but to look after the little needs of little children? And God, our Father, is a good father. He pities us as fathers pity their children and condescends to us. He knows the number of the stars, and calls them all by their names, yet He heals the broken in heart and binds up their wounds. The same God who kindles the sun has said, "I will not quench the smoking flax." If you have but confidence in God, you will take your great things and your little things to Him and He will never belie your confidence-for He has said they that trust in Him shall never be ashamed or confused, world without end. Faith must succeed.

But next, love must succeed, too, since we have already seen that the man who loves, in the Christian sense, is in accord with God. If you confine your love to your own family, you must not expect God to do so, and prayers narrowed within that circle He will disregard. If a man loves his own little self and hopes everybody's crop of wheat will fail, that his own produce may fetch a higher price, he certainly cannot expect the Lord to agree with such mean selfishness. If a man has heart enough to embrace all the creatures of God in his affection while he yet prays specially for the household of faith, his prayers will be after the divine mind. His love and God's goodness run side by side. Though God's love is like a mighty rolling river and his is like a trickling brook, yet they both run in the same direction and will both come to the same end. God always hears the prayers of a loving man because those prayers are the shadows of His own decrees.

Again, the man of obedience is the man whom God will hear because his obedient heart leads him to pray humbly and with submission, for he feels it to be his highest desire that the Lord's will should be done. Hence it is that the man of obedient heart prays like an oracle; his prayers are prophecies. Is he not one with God? Does he not desire and ask for exactly what God intends? How can a prayer shot from such a bow ever fail to reach its target?

If your soul gets into accord with God's soul, you will wish God's own wishes. The difficulty is that we do not keep, as the word is, in rapport with God. But if we did, then we should strike the same note as God strikes and though His would sound like thunder and ours as a whisper, yet there would be a perfect unison-the note struck by prayer on earth would coincide with that which sounds forth from the decrees in heaven.

Again, the man who lives in fellowship with God will assuredly prevail in prayer because, if he dwells in God, and God dwells in him, he will desire what God desires. The believer in communion with the Lord desires man's good and so does God. He desires Christ's glory and so does God. He desires the church's prosperity and so does God. He desires himself to be a pattern of holiness and God desires it too. If that man at any time has a desire which is not according to God's will, it is the result of ignorance, seeing that man is but man and not God. Even when he is at the best he must err, but he provides for this defect by the form of his prayer which always has this addendum at the end of it-"Lord, if I have asked in this, my prayer, for anything which is not according to Your mind, I beseech You, do not regard me. And if any wish which I have expressed to You-even though it is the desire which burns in my bosom above all other wishes-is a wish that is not right in Your sight, regard me not, my Father, but, in Your infinite love and compassion, do something better for Your servant than Your servant knows how to ask." Now, when a prayer is after that fashion, how can it fail? The Lord looks out of the windows of heaven and sees such a prayer coming to Him, just as Noah saw the dove returning to the ark, and He puts out His hand to that prayer. And as Noah plucked the dove into the ark, so does God pluck that prayer in unto Him and puts it into His own bosom, and says, "You came out of My bosom, and I welcome you back to Me: My Spirit composed you, therefore will I answer you."

And here, again, let us say, our text speaks of the Christian man as being filled with God's Spirit: "We know that He abides in us, by the Spirit which He has given us." Who knows the mind of a man but the spirit of a man? So, who knows the things of God but the Spirit of God? And if the Spirit of God dwells in us, then He tells us what God's mind is. He makes intercession in the saints according to the will of God. It is sometimes imagined that men who have prevalence in prayer can pray for what they like, but I can assure you any one of these will tell you that that is not so. You may call upon such a man and ask him to pray for you, but he cannot promise that he will. There are strange holdings back to such men when they feel they know not how or why that they cannot pray effectual fervent prayers in certain cases, though they might desire to do so. Like Paul, when he essayed to go into Bithynia and the Spirit suffered him not, so there are requests which we would naturally like to put up, but we are bound in spirit. There may apparently be nothing objectionable about the prayer, but the secret of the Lord is with them that fear Him and He gives secret intimations when and where His chosen may hope to prevail. He gives you the promise that He will hear your believing prayer, you being a man that walks with Him, filled with His Spirit. But He does not, at the same time, give you faith about everything that everybody likes to put before you-on the contrary He gives you a discretion, a judgment and a wisdom-and the Spirit makes intercession in the saints according to the will of God.

Thus I think I have laid down the doctrine pretty clearly. Now a few minutes of practical improvement, as the old Puritans used to say. I only wish it may be of improvement to many of us.

The first is, we want to pray for a great blessing as a church. I think I should command your votes if I said we intend to pray God to send a blessing on the church at large. Very well, have we the essentials for success? Do we believing in the name of Jesus Christ? Well, I think we are. I do not think fault could be found with the soundness of our faith, though much is to be confessed about the weakness of it. Let us pass on to the next question. Are we full of love to God and one another? The double commandment is that we believe on the name of Jesus Christ and that we love one another. Do we love one another? Are we walking in love? There are none of us perfect in it. I will begin to confess by acknowledging I am not what I should be in that respect. Will you let the confession go round and each one think how often we have done unloving things, thought unloving things, said unloving things, listened to unloving gossip, held back our hand unlovingly when we ought to have rendered help and put forth our hand unlovingly to push down a man who was falling? If in the church of God there is a lack of love, we cannot expect prayer to be heard, for God will say, "You ask for prosperity. What for? To add more to a community which does not already love itself? You ask for conversions. What? Is it to bring in others to join an unloving community?" Do you expect God to save sinners whom you do not love, and to convert souls whom you do not care a bit about? We must love souls into Christ for, under God's Holy Spirit, the great instrument for the conquest of the world is love. If Christians will love more than Muslims do, and Jews do, they will overcome Muslims and Jews. And if they show less love, Muslims and Jews will overcome them. The sword of the Spirit, which is the Word of God, is the master weapon, and next to that is the loving carriage and generous conversation of Christians towards their fellow men. How much of that have we got? Shall I say, how little?

Next, are we doing that which is pleasing in God's sight? We cannot expect answers to prayer if we are not. Put the inquiry to yourselves all round. Let each church member, especially, answer that question. Have you been doing, lately, that which you would like Jesus Christ to see? Is your household ordered in such a way that it pleases God? Suppose Jesus Christ had visited your house this week, uninvited and unexpected: what would He have thought of that which He would have seen? "Oh," says one, "I know so-and-so acts very inconsistently." Sir, I pray you think of yourself! That is the point. Correct yourself. Unless the members of God's church do that which is pleasing in His sight, they bar the door against prosperity; they prevent the prayers of the church from succeeding. Who wishes to be the man that stands in the way of the prosperity of God's church through inconsistency of conduct? Who would be so guilty? God forgive some of you. We could speak of some even weeping, for, alas, though they profess to be the followers of Christ, they are so inconsistent that they are not friends, but enemies of the cross of Christ.

The next question is, do we dwell in God? The text says that if we keep His commandments, God dwells in us, and we in Him. Is that so? I mean, during the day do we think of God? In our business are we still with God? A Christian is not to run unto God in the morning and again at night, and use Him as a shelter and a makeshift, as people do of an arch or a portico which they run under in a shower of rain. We are to dwell in God and live in Him from the rising of the sun until the going down thereof, making Him our daily meditation, and walking as in His sight, feeling evermore, "You God see me." How is it with you, dear friends! O let the question go from pew to pew and heart to heart, and mind-let each one answer for himself.

Lastly, does the Spirit of God actuate us, or is it another spirit? Do we wait upon God and say, "Lord, let Your Spirit tell me what to say in this case, and what to do. Rule my judgment, subdue my passions, keep down my baser impulses and let Your Spirit guide me. Lord, be You to me better than myself. Be soul and life to me and in the triple kingdom of my spirit, soul, and body, good Lord, be You supreme Master that in every province of my nature Your law may be set up and Your will may be regarded"? We would have a mighty church, if we were all, of this mind. But the mixed multitude, are with us, and the mixed multitude that came out of Egypt and these fall a-lusting. The mischief always begins with them. God save us as a church from losing His presence! The mixed multitude must be with us to try us, for the Lord has said, "Let both grow together till the harvest," and if we try to root up the tares we should root up the wheat also-yet, at any rate, let us pray God to make the wheat be the stronger. One of two things always happens in a church. Either the wheat chokes the weeds or the weeds choke the wheat. God grant that the wheat may overtop the weeds in our case! God grant grace to His servants to be strong enough to overcome the evil which surrounds them, and having done all, to stand to the praise of the glory of His grace, who also has made us accepted in the Beloved. The Lord bless you, and be with you evermore. Amen and Amen.

Chapter 4
THE POWER OF PRAYER AND THE PLEASURE OF PRAISE

"You also helping together by prayer for us, that for the gift bestowed
upon us by the means of many persons, thanks may be given by many on
our behalf. For our rejoicing in this, the testimony of our conscience, that
in simplicity and godly sincerity, not with fleshly wisdom, but by the grace
of God, we have had our conversation in the world
and more abundantly to you."
2 Corinthians 1:11, 12.

THE apostle Paul had, by singular providences, been delivered from imminent peril in Asia. During the great riot at Ephesus, when Demetrius and his fellow shrine-makers raised a great tumult against him, because they saw that their craft was in danger, Paul's life was greatly in jeopardy. Consequently he writes, "We were pressed out of measure, above strength, insomuch that we despaired even of life." The apostle attributes to God, alone, his singular preservation; and if he referred also to the occasion when he was stoned and left for dead, there is much appropriateness in his blessing "God which raised the dead." The apostle, moreover, argues from the fact that God had thus delivered him in the past, and was still his helper in the present, that He would be with him also in the future! Paul is a master at all arithmetic. His faith was always a ready-reckoner. We here find him computing by the believer's Rule of Three; he argues from the past to the present and from the present to things yet to come. The verse preceding our text is a brilliant example of this arriving at a comfortable conclusion by the Rule of Three- "Who delivered us from so great a death, and does deliver: in whom we trust that He will yet deliver us." Because our God is "the same yesterday, today, and forever," His love in time past is an infallible assurance of His kindness today, and an equally certain pledge of His faithfulness on the morrow; whatever our circumstances may be, however perplexed may be our pathway, and however dark our horizon, if we argue by the rule of, "He has, He does, He will," our comfort can never be destroyed! Courage, then, O you afflicted seed of Israel; if you had a changeable God to deal with, your souls might be full of bitterness-but because He is, "the same yesterday, today, and forever," every repeated manifestation of His grace should make it more easy for you to rest upon Him! Every renewed experience of His fidelity should confirm your confidence in His grace. May the most blessed Spirit teach us to grow in holy confidence in our ever faithful Lord.

Although our apostle thus acknowledged God's hand and God's hand alone, in his deliverance, yet he was not so foolish as to deny or undervalue the second causes. On the contrary, having first praised the God of all comfort, he now remembers with gratitude the earnest prayers of the many loving intercessors. Gratitude to God must never become an excuse for ingratitude to man! It is true that Jehovah shielded the apostle of the Gentiles, but He did it in answer to prayer; the chosen vessel was not broken by the rod of the wicked, for the outstretched hand of the God of heaven was his defense-but that hand was outstretched because the people of Corinth, and the saints of God everywhere had prevailed at the throne of grace by their united supplications! With gratitude, those successful pleadings are mentioned in the text, "You also helping together by prayer for us," and he desires the brothers and sisters now to unite their praises with his, "that for the gift bestowed upon us by the means of many persons, thanks may be given by many on our behalf." He adds that he has a claim upon their love since he was not as some who were unfaithful to their trust, but his conscience was clear that he had preached the Word simply and with sincerity.

While speaking upon these topics, may the anointing Spirit now descend to make them profitable to us! We shall, first, acknowledge the power of united prayer; secondly, excite you to united praise; and then, in the third place, urge our joyful claim upon you-a claim which is not ours alone, but belongs to all ministers of God who in sincerity labor for souls.

I. First, then, dear friends, it is my duty and my privilege this morning to ACKNOWLEDGE THE POWER OF UNITED PRAYER.

It has pleased God to make prayer the abounding and rejoicing river through which most of our choice mercies flow to us. It is the golden key which unlocks the well-stored granaries of our heavenly Joseph. It is written upon each of the mercies of the covenant, "For this will I be inquired of by the house of Israel to do it for them." There are mercies which come unsought, for God is found of them that sought not for Him, but there are other favors which are only bestowed upon the men who ask, and therefore receive-who seek, and therefore find-who knock, and therefore gain an entrance. Why God has been pleased to command us to pray at all it is not difficult to discover, for prayer glorifies God, by putting man in the most humble posture of worship! The creature in prayer acknowledges his Creator with reverence, and confesses Him to be the giver of every good and perfect gift; the eyes are lifted up to behold the glory of the Lord, while the knees are bent to the earth in the lowliness of acknowledged weakness. Though prayer is not the highest mode of adoration, or otherwise it would be continued by the saints in heaven, yet, it is the most humble, and so the most fitting to set forth the glory of the perfect One as it is beheld by imperfect flesh and blood. From the "Our Father," in which we claim relationship, right on to, "the kingdom and the power and the glory," which we ascribe to the only true God, every sentence of prayer honors the Most High! The groans and tears of humble petitioners are as truly acceptable as the continual, "Holy, holy, holy," of the Cherubim and Seraphim; for in their very essence, all truthful confessions of personal fault are but homage paid to the infinite perfections of the Lord of hosts. More honored is the Lord by our prayers than by the unceasing smoke of the holy incense of the altar which stood before the veil. Moreover, the act of prayer teaches us our unworthiness, which is no small blessing to such proud beings as we are. If God gave us favors without compelling us to pray for them, we would never know how poor we are, but a true prayer is an inventory of needs, a catalog of necessities, a request in forma pauperis, an exposure of secret wounds, a revelation of hidden poverty. While it is an application to divine wealth, it is a confession of human emptiness. I believe that the most healthy state of a Christian is to be always empty, and always depending upon the Lord for supplies; to be always poor in self and rich in Jesus; weak as water personally, but mighty through God to do great exploits; and therefore the use of prayer, because while it adores God, it lays the creature where he should be in the very dust. Prayer is in itself, apart from the answer which it brings, a great benefit to the Christian. As the runner gains strength for the race by daily exercise, so for the great race of life, we acquire energy by the hallowed labor of prayer. Prayer plumes the wings of God's young eaglets that they may learn to mount above the clouds! Prayer girds the loins of

God's warriors, and sends them forth to combat with their sinews braced, and their muscles firm. An earnest pleader comes out of his closet, even as the sun rises from the chambers of the east, rejoicing like a strong man to run his race; prayer is that uplifted hand of Moses which routs the Amalekites more than the sword of Joshua; it is the arrow shot from the chamber of the prophet foreboding defeat to the Syrians. What if I say that prayer clothes the believer with the attributes of Deity, girds human weakness with divine strength, turns human folly into heavenly wisdom, and gives to troubled mortals the serenity of the immortal God? I know not what prayer cannot do! I thank You, great God, for the mercy seat, a choice gift of Your marvelous loving-kindness. Help us to use it aright!

As many mercies are conveyed from heaven in the ship of prayer, so there are many choice and special favors which can only be brought to us by the fleets of united prayer. Many are the good things which God will give to His lonely Elijahs and Daniels, but if two of you agree as touching anything that you shall ask, there is no limit to God's bountiful answers. Peter might never have been brought out of prison if it had not been that prayer was made without ceasing by all the Church for him! Pentecost might never have come if all the disciples had not been, "with one accord in one place," waiting for the descent of the tongues of fire. God is pleased to give many mercies to one pleader, but at times He seems to say, "You shall all appear before Me and entreat My favor, for I will not see your face unless even your younger brothers and sisters are with you." Why is this, dear friends? I take it that thus our gracious Lord sets forth His own esteem for the communion of saints. "I believe in the communion of saints" is one article of the great Christian creed, but how few there are who understand it! Oh, there is such a thing as real union among God's people. We may be called by different names- "But all the servants of our King In heaven and earth are one!" We cannot afford to lose the help and love of our brothers and sisters. Augustine says, "The poor are made for the rich, and the rich are made for the poor." I do not doubt but that strong saints are made for weak saints, and that the weak saints bring special benedictions upon the full grown believers. There is fitness in the whole body-each joint owes something to every other- and the whole body is bound together and compacted by that which every joint supplies. There are certain glands in the human body which the anatomist hardly understands. He can say of the liver, for instance, that it yields a very valuable fluid of the utmost value in the bodily economy. But there are other secretions whose distinct value he cannot ascertain. Yet, doubtless, if that gland were removed, the whole body might suffer to a high degree! And so, beloved friends, there may be some believers of whom we may say, "I do not know the use of them; I cannot tell what good that Christian does;" yet, were that insignificant, and apparently useless member removed, the whole body might be made to suffer, the whole frame might become sick, and the whole heart faint! This is probably the reason why many a weighty gift of heaven's love is only granted to combined petitioning, that we may perceive the use of the whole body, and so may be compelled to recognize the real vital union which divine grace has made-and daily maintains among the people of God. Is it not a happy thought, dear friends, that the very poorest and most obscure Church member can add something to the body's strength? We cannot all preach; we cannot all rule; we cannot all give gold and silver, but we can all contribute our prayers! There is no convert, though he is but two or three days old in divine grace, who cannot pray! There is no bedridden sister in Jesus who cannot pray! There is no sick, aged, imbecile, obscure, illiterate, or penniless believer who cannot add his supplications to the general stock! This is the Church's riches! We put boxes at the door that we may receive your offerings to God's cause-remember, there is a spiritual chest within the Church into which we should all drop our loving intercessions, as into the treasury of the Lord. Even the widow without her two mites can give her offering to this treasury! See, then, dear friends, what union and communion there are among the people of God, since there are certain mercies which are only bestowed while the saints unitedly pray. How we ought to feel this bond of union! How we ought to pray for one another! How, as often as the Church meets together for supplication, should we all make it our bounded duty to be there! I would that some of you who are absent from the prayer meeting upon any little excuse would reflect how much you rob us all. The prayer meeting is an invaluable institution, ministering strength to all other meetings and agencies. Are there not many of you who might, by a little pinching of your time, and pressing of your labors, come among us a little more often? And what if you should lose a customer now and then, do you not think that this loss could be well made up to you by your gains on other days? Or if not so, would not the spiritual profit much more than counterbalance any little temporal loss? "Not forgetting the assembling of yourselves together as the manner of some is."

We are now prepared for a further observation. This united prayer should especially be made for the ministers of God. It is for them, peculiarly, that this public prayer is intended. Paul asks for it- "Brethren, pray for us." And all God's ministers, to the latest time, will always confess that this is the secret source of their strength. The prayers of the people must be the might of the ministers. Shall I try to show you why the minister, more than any other man in the Church, needs the earnest prayers of the people? Is not his position the most perilous? Satan's orders to the hosts of hell are, "Fight neither with small nor great, but only with the ministers of God." He knows if he can once smite through the heart of one of these, there will be a general confusion, for if the champion is dead, then the people flee! It is around the standard-bearer that the fight is thickest. There the battle-axes ring upon the helmets; there the arrows are bent upon the armor, for the enemy knows that if he can cut down the standard, or cleave the skull of its bearer, he will strike a heavy blow and cause deep discouragement. Press around us, then, you men at arms! Knights of the red cross, rally for our defense, for the fight grows hot! We beseech you, if you elect us to the office of the ministry, stand fast at our side in our hourly conflicts! I noticed on returning from Rotterdam, when we were crossing the bar at the mouth of the Maas, where by reason of a deep tide and a bad wind, the navigation was exceedingly dangerous, that orders were issued-"All hands on deck!" So I think the life of a minister is so perilous, that I may well cry, "All hands on deck"-every man to prayer! Let even the weakest saint become instant in supplication! The minister, standing in such a perilous position, has, moreover, a solemn weight of responsibility resting on him. Every man should be his brother's keeper in a measure, but woe to the watchmen of God if they are not faithful, for at their hands shall the blood of souls be required; at their door shall God lay the ruin of men if they preach not the gospel fully and faithfully. There are times when this burden of the Lord weighs upon God's ministers until they cry out in pain as if their hearts would burst with anguish. I marked the captain as we crossed that bar throwing the lead, himself, into the sea; and when one asked why he did not let the sailors do it, he said, "At this point, just now, I dare not trust any man but myself to heave the lead, for we have hardly six inches between our ship and the bottom." And, indeed, we felt the vessel touch once or twice most unpleasantly. So there will come times with every preacher of the gospel-if he is what he should be-when he will be in dread suspense for his hearers, and he will not be able to discharge his duty by proxy, but must personally labor for men, not even trusting himself to preach but calling upon his God for help, since he is now overwhelmed with the burden of men's souls. Oh, do pray for us! If God gives us to you, and if you accept the gift most cheerfully, do not so despise both God and us as to leave us penniless and poverty-stricken because your prayers are withheld!

Moreover, the preservation of the minister is one of the most important objectives to the Church. You may lose a sailor from the ship, and that is very bad, both for him and for you, but if the pilot should fall over, or the captain should be smitten with sickness or the helmsman be washed from the wheel, then what is the vessel to do? Therefore, though prayer is to be put up for every other person in the Church, yet for the minister is it to be offered first and foremost, because of the position which he occupies. And then, how much more is asked of him than of you? If you are to keep a private table for individual instruction, he is, as it were, to keep a public table, a feast of good things for all comers; and how shall he do this unless his Master gives him rich provisions? You are to shine as a candle in a house, the minister has to be as a lighthouse to be seen far across the deep and how shall he shine the whole night long unless he is trimmed by his Master, and fresh oil is given him from heaven? His influence is wider than yours if it is for evil, he shall be a deadly upas, with spreading boughs poisoning all beneath his shadow; but if God makes him a star in His right hand, his ray of light shall cheer with its genial influence whole nations, and whole periods of time! If there is any truth in all this, I implore you, yield us generously and constantly the assistance of your prayers.

I find that in the original, the word for, "helping together," implies very earnest WORK. Some people's prayers have no work in them, but the only prayer which prevails with God is a real working- man's prayer-where the petitioner, like a Samson, shakes the gates of mercy, and labors to pull them up rather than be denied an entrance! We do not want fingertip prayers, which only touch the burden, we need shoulder prayers which bear a load of earnestness, and are not to be denied their desire. We do not want those dainty runaway knocks at the door of mercy, which professors give when they show off at prayer meetings, but we ask for the knocking of a man who means to have, and means to stop at mercy's gate till it opens and all his needs shall be supplied! The energetic, vehement violence of the man who is not to be denied, but intends to carry heaven by storm until he wins his heart's desire. This is the prayer which ministers covet of their people!

Melancthon, it is said, derived great comfort from the information that certain poor weavers, women and children, had met together to pray for the Reformation. Yes, Melancthon there was solid ground for comfort here. Depend on it, it was not only Luther, but the thousands of poor persons who sung psalms at the plow-tail, and the hundreds of serving men and women who offered supplications, that made the Reformation what it was. We are told of Paulus Phagius, a celebrated Hebrew scholar, very useful in introducing the Reformation into this country, that one of his frequent requests of his younger scholars was that they would continue in prayer, so that God might be pleased to pour out a blessing in answer to them. Have I not said a hundred times that all the blessings that God has given us here, all the increase to our Church, has been due, under God, to your earnest, fervent supplications? There have been heaven-moving seasons both in this house and at New Park Street. We have had times when we have felt we could die sooner than not be heard; when we carried our Church on our bosom as a mother carries her child; when we felt a yearning and a travailing in birth for the souls of men! We may truly say, when we see our Church daily increasing, and the multitudes still hanging upon our lips to listen to the Word, "What has God worked?" Shall we now cease from our prayers? Shall we now say unto the Great High Priest, "It is enough"? Shall we now pluck the glowing coals from the altar, and quench the burning incense? Shall we now refuse to bring the morning and evening lambs of prayer and praise to the sacrifice? O children of Ephraim, being armed and carrying bows, will you turn your backs in the day of battle? The flood is divided before you; the Jordan is driven back! Will you refuse to march through the depths? God, even your God, goes up before you! The shout of a King is heard in the midst of your hosts! Will you now be cowardly and refuse to go up and possess the land? Will you now lose your first love? Shall "Ichabod" be written upon the forefront of this tabernacle? Shall it be said that God has forsaken you? Shall the day come in which the daughters of Philistia shall rejoice, and the sons of Syria shall triumph? If not, to your knees again, with all the force of prayer! If not, to your vehement supplications once more! If not, if you would not see good blighted, and evil triumphant, clasp hands again and in the name of Him who always lives to intercede once more be prevalent in prayer that the blessing may again descend! "You also helping together by prayer for us."

II. We must now EXCITE YOU TO PRAISE.

Praise should always follow answered prayer; the mist of earth's gratitude should rise as the sun of heaven's love warms the ground. Has the Lord been gracious to you, and inclined His ear to the voice of your supplication? Then praise Him as long as you live! Deny not a song to Him who has answered your prayer, and given you the desire of your heart. To be silent over God's mercies is to incur the guilt of shocking ingratitude, and ingratitude is one of the worst of crimes. I trust, dear friends, you will not act as basely as the nine lepers, who after they had been healed of their leprosy, returned not to give thanks unto the healing Lord. To forget to praise God is to refuse to benefit ourselves, for praise, like prayer, is exceedingly useful to the spiritual man. It is a high and healthful exercise. To dance, like David, before the Lord, is to quicken the blood in the veins, and make the pulse beat at a healthier rate. Praise gives to us a great feast, like that of Solomon, who gave to every man a good piece of meat, and a flagon of wine. Praise is the most heavenly of Christian duties! The angels pray not, but they cease not to praise both day and night. To bless God for mercies received is to benefit our fellow men-"The humble shall hear thereof and be glad." Others who have been in like circumstances shall take comfort if we can say, "Oh, magnify the Lord with me, and let us exalt His name together, this poor man cried, and the Lord heard him!" Tongue-tied Christians are a sad dishonor to the Church. We have some such, some whom the devil has gagged and the loudest music they ever make is when they are champing the bit of their silence. I would, my brothers and sisters, that in all such cases the tongue of the dumb may sing.

To go a step further here, as praise is good and pleasant, blessing man and glorifying God, united praise has a very special commendation. United praise is like music in concert. The sound of one instrument is exceedingly sweet, but when hundreds of instruments, both wind and stringed, are all combined, then the orchestra sends forth a noble volume of harmony! The praise of one Christian is accepted before God like a grain of incense, but the praise of many is like a censor full of frankincense smoking up before the Lord. Combined praise is an anticipation of heaven, for in that general assembly they all, together, with one heart and voice, praise the Lord- "Ten thousand thousand are their tongues, But all their joys are one!" Public praise is very agreeable to the Christian himself. How many burdens has it removed? I am sure when I hear the shout of praise in this house, it warms my heart. It is at times a little too slow for my taste, and I must urge you to quicken your pace, that the rolling waves of majestic praise may display their full force! Yet with all drawbacks, to my heart, there is no music like yours. My Dutch friends praise the Lord so very slowly that one might very well go to sleep, lulled by their lengthened strains. Even there, however, the many voices make a grand harmony of praise! I love to hear God's people sing when they really do sing, not when it is a drawing out somewhere between harmony and discord. O for a sacred song, a shout of lofty praise in which every man's soul beats the time, and every man's tongue sounds the tune and each singer feels a high ambition to excel his fellow in gratitude and love! There is something exceedingly delightful in the union of true hearts in the worship of God and when these hearts are expressed in song, how sweet the charming sounds! I think we ought to have a praise meeting once a week. We have a prayer meeting every Monday, and a prayer meeting every Saturday, and a prayer meeting every morning, but why do we not have a praise meeting? Surely seasons should be set apart for services made up of praise from beginning to end. Let us try the plan at once.

As I said about united prayer, that it should be offered especially for ministers, so should united praise often take the same aspect. The whole company should praise and bless God for the mercy rendered to the Church through its pastors. Hear how our apostle puts it again "That for the gift bestowed upon us by the means of many persons, thanks may be given by many on our behalf." brothers and sisters, we ought to praise God for good ministers that they live, for when they die, much of their work dies with them. It is astonishing how a reformation will press on while Luther and Calvin live, and how it will cease as soon as the reformers die! The spirits of good men are immortal only in a sense. The Churches of God in this age are like the Israelites in the times of the judges, when the judges died they went after graven images again. And it is so now. While God spares the man, the Church prospers, but when the man dies, the zeal which he blew to a flame smolders among the ashes in nine cases out of ten, if not in 99 out of every hundred! The prosperity of a Church rests on the minister's life. God so ordains it to humble us. There should be gratitude, then, for spared life; but there should be great gratitude for preserved character, for oh, when a minister falls, what a disgrace it is! Why, when you read in the police reports the sad case of the Rev. Mr.   , who chose to call himself a Baptist minister, everybody said, "What a shocking thing! What a bad set the Baptists must be!" Now, any fool in the world may call himself a Baptist minister! Our liberty is so complete that no law or order exists. Any man who can get a dozen to listen to him preach is a minister, at least to them; therefore, you cannot suppose but what there will be some hypocrites who will take the name in order to get some sort of reputation. If the true minister is kept, and made to hold fast his integrity, there should be constant gratitude to God on his behalf. If the minister is kept well supplied with goodly matter; if he is like a springing well; if God gives him to bring out of His treasury things both new and old to feed His people, there should be hearty thanks. And if he is kept sound, if he goes not aside to philosophy on the one hand, nor to a narrowness of doctrine on the other, there should be thanksgiving there. If God gives to the masses the will to hear him, and above all, if souls are converted and saints are edified, there should be never-ceasing honor and praise to God! Ah, I am talking now about what you all know, and you just nod your heads to it, and think there is not much in it, but if you were made to live in Holland for a little time, you would soon appreciate these remarks. While traveling there, I stayed in houses with godly men-men of God with whom I could hold sweet communion-who cannot attend what was once their place of worship. Why not? "Sir," they say, "can I go to a place of worship when the most of the ministers deny every Word of Scripture? Not those of the Reformed Church only, but of every sect in Holland! How can I listen to the traitors who swear to the Calvinistic or Lutheran articles, and then go into the pulpit and deny the reality of the resurrection, or assert that the ascension of Jesus is a mere spiritual parable?"

I find that in the Netherlands, they are 50 years in advance of us in infidelity! We shall soon catch up with them if gentlemen of a certain school I know of are allowed to multiply. The Dutch divines have taken great strides in Neologism, till now the people love the truth of God, and there are multitudes who are willing to hear it, but these are compelled absolutely to refuse to go to church at all, lest by any means they should give countenance to the heretical and false doctrines which are preached to them every Sunday! Ah, if God were once to take away from England the ministers who preach the gospel boldly and plainly, you would cry to God to give you the candlestick back again! We may indeed say of England- "With all your faults I love you still."

We have a colonial bishop who avows his unbelief; we have a few men of all denominations who are quietly sliding from the truth; but thank God they are nothing as of yet; they are but as a drop in a bucket compared to the Churches of Christ, and those among us who are not quite as Calvinistic as we might wish, I thank God, never dispute the Inspiration of Scripture, nor doubt the great truth of justification by faith. We have still preserved among us men who are faithful to God, and preach the whole truth as it is in Jesus! Be thankful for your ministers, I say again, for if you were placed where some believers are, you would cry out to your God "Lord, send us back Your prophets; send us a famine of bread or a famine of water, but send us not a famine of the Word of God!"

I ask for myself this morning, as your minister, your thanksgivings to be mingled with mine in praising God for the help which He has given to me in the very arduous work of the last fortnight. Praise be to God for the acceptance which He gave me in that country among all ranks of the people. I speak to His praise and not to mine, for this has been a vow with me, that if God will give me a harvest, I will not have an ear of corn of it, but He shall have it all! I found, in all the places where I went, great multitudes of people, crowds who could not understand the preacher, but who wanted to see his face, because God had blessed his translated sermons to their souls! Multitudes gave me the grip of brotherly kindness and, with tears in their eyes, invoked, in the Dutch language, every blessing upon my head. I hoped to preach to some fifties and hundreds, and instead of that, there were so many that the great cathedrals were not too large! This surprised me, and made me glad and caused me to rejoice in God and I ask you to rejoice with me. I thank God for the acceptance which He gave me among all ranks of the people. While the poor crowded to shake hands, till they almost pulled me in pieces, it pleased God to move the heart of the Queen of Holland to send for me, and for an hour and a quarter, I was privileged to talk with her concerning the things which make for our peace. I sought no interview with her, but it was her own wish; and then I lifted up my soul to God that I might talk of nothing but Christ, and might preach to her of nothing but Jesus; and so it pleased the Master to help me, and I left that very amiable lady, not having shunned to declare the whole counsel of God! Gratified was I, indeed, to find myself received cordially by all denominations, so that on the Saturday at Amsterdam, I preached in the Mennonite Church in the morning, and at the Old Dutch Reformed Church in the evening; the next Sunday morning in the English Presbyterian Church, and then again, in the evening, in the Dutch Free Church. Sometimes I was allowed to preach in the great cathedrals, as in the Dom Kirk at Utrecht, and in Peter's Kirk, at Leyden, not having the poor only, but the nobility and the gentry of the land, who, of course, could understand English better than most of the poor, who have had no opportunity of learning it. I felt, while going from town to town, the Master helping me continually to preach. I never knew such elasticity of spirit, such bounding of heart in my life before, and I come back, not wearied and tired, though preaching twice every day, but fuller of strength and vigor than when I first set out! I give God the glory for the many souls I have heard of who have been converted through the reading of the printed sermons, and for the loving blessings of those who followed us to the water's edge with many tears, saying to us-"Do your diligence to come again before winter," and urging us once more to preach the Word in that land. There may be mingled with this some touch of egotism; the Lord knows whether it is so or not, but I am not conscious of it. I do praise and bless His name, that in a land where there is so much philosophy, He has helped me to preach His truth so simply, that I never uttered a word as a mere doctrinalist, but I preached Christ and nothing but Christ! Rejoice with me, my dear brothers and sisters! I must have you rejoice in it, or if you will not, I must rejoice alone, but my loaf of praise is too great for me to eat it all!

III. And we come to a close. I have to urge THE JOYFUL CLAIMS which the apostle gives in the 12th verse, as a reason WHY THERE SHOULD BE PRAYER AND PRAISE.

"For our rejoicing is this, the testimony of our conscience, that in simplicity and godly sincerity, not with fleshly wisdom, but by the grace of God, we have had our conversation in the world, and more abundantly to you." Ah, after all, a man's comfort must come, next to the finished salvation of God, from the testimony of his own conscience! And to a minister, what a testimony it is that he has preached the gospel in simplicity, to which there are two senses-preached it not with double-mindedness- saying one thing and meaning another. And he has preached it, not as oarsmen row-looking one way and pulling another but preached it meaning what he said, having a single heart, desiring God's glory and the salvation of men! What a blessing to have preached it simply, that is to say, without hard words, without polished phrases, never studying elocutionary graces, never straining after oratorical embellishments! How accursed must be the life of a man who profanes the pulpit to the dignity of eloquence! How desperate will be his deathbed when he remembers that he made an exhibition of his powers of speech rather than of the solid things which make for the winning of souls! That conscience may well be easy that can speak of having dealt with God's truth in simplicity. The apostle also says that he had preached it with sincerity, that is, he had preached it meaning it, feeling it preached it so that none could accuse him of being false! The Greek word has something in it of sunlight, and he is the true minister of God who preaches what he would wish to have hung up in the sunlight, or who has the sunlight shining right through him. I am afraid we are none of us like white glass, most of us are colored a little, but he is happy who seeks to get rid of the coloring matter as much as possible, so that the light of the gospel may shine right straight, clear as it comes from the Sun of Righteousness, through him! Paul had preached with simplicity and sincerity. And he adds, "Not with fleshly wisdom." Oh, what stories have I heard of what fleshly wisdom will do! And I have learned a lesson during the last fortnight which I would that England would learn. There are three schools of theological error over yonder, and each one leaps over the back of its fellow. Some of them hold that all the facts of Scripture are only myths; others of them say that there are some good things in the Bible, though there are a great many mistakes; and others go still further, and fling the whole Bible away altogether as to its inspiration, though they still preach it, and still lean on it, saying that they do that merely for the edification of the vulgar-merely holding it up for the sake of the masses-though I ought to add merely to get their living as well. Sad! Sad! Sad that the Church has gone to such a length as that-the Old Dutch Reformed Church-the very mirror of Calvinism, standing fast and firm in its creeds to all the doctrines we love, and yet gone astray to latitudinarian and licentious liberty! Oh, how earnestly should we decry fleshly wisdom! I am afraid, dear friends, that sometimes some of you, when you hear a minister, you like him to put it pretty well, and you find fault unless he shows some degree of talent. I wonder whether that is not a sin? I am half inclined to think it is. I sometimes think whether we ought not to look less every day to talent, and more and more to the matter of the gospel that is preached; whether if a man is blessed with elocutionary power we may, perhaps, be more profited by him whether that is not a weakness, whether we had not better go back to the days of fishermen once again, and give men no sort of education whatever, but just send them to preach the truth of God simply, rather than go the length they are now going, giving men I know not what, of all sorts of learning that is of no earthly use to them, but which only helps them to pervert the simplicity of God. I love that word in my text "Not with fleshly wisdom."

And now I lay my claim, as my conscience bears me witness, I lay my claim to this boasting of our apostle. I have preached God's gospel in simplicity; I do not know how I can preach it more simply, nor can I more honestly declare it. I have preached it sincerely-the Searcher of all hearts knows that-and I have not preached it with fleshly wisdom, and that for one excellent reason-that I have not any-and have been compelled to keep to the simple testimony of the Lord! But if I have done anything, it has been done by the grace of God. If any success has been achieved, it has been divine grace that has done it all. "And more especially to you," for though our word has gone forth to many lands, and our testimony belts the globe, yet, "more especially to you." You have we warned; you have we entreated; you have we exhorted; with you have we pleaded; over you have we wept; for you have we prayed; to some of you, we have been a spiritual parent in Christ; to many of you, as a nursing father; to many of you, as a teacher and an edifier in the gospel; and we hope to all of you, a sincere friend in Christ Jesus! Therefore, do I claim your prayers-yours more than any other people's; and though there will be not a few who will remember us in their supplications, I do implore you, inasmuch as it has been, "especially to you," let me especially have your prayers! Some will say that it is unkind even for me to suppose that you do not pray. Well, I do not so suppose it out of unkindness, but there may be some who forget- some who forget to plead. Oh, do still pray for me! The whole congregation is not saved yet; there are some who hear us who are not yet converted. Plead with God for their sakes! There are some hard hearts unbroken; ask God to make the hammer strike; and while there are some still unmelted, pray God to make the Word like a fire! This great London needs to be stirred from end to end! Pray for all your ministers, that God may make them mighty! The Church needs still more of the loud voice of God to wake it from its sleep! Ask God to bless all His sent servants. Plead with Him with divine energy, that so His kingdom may come, and His will may be done on earth as it is in heaven!

O that you all believed in Jesus! For until you do, you cannot pray nor praise! O that you all believed in Jesus! Remember, this is the only way of salvation. Trust Jesus, for he who believes on Him is not condemned, but he who believes not is condemned already, because he believes not on the Son of God. Trust Jesus and you shall be saved. May Christ accept you now, for His own love's sake. Amen.

Printed in Great Britain
by Amazon

18398849R00038